How I Got Over

Testimonies of African Americans
Reflections on the Books of Job and Psalms
Bible Study Applications

Editor
Colleen Birchett, Ph.D.

URBAN MINISTRIES, INC.
chicago, il 60643

Publisher
Urban Ministries, Inc.
1350 West 103rd Street
Chicago, Illinois 60643
(312) 233-4499

First Edition
First Printing
ISBN: 0-940955-26-1
Catalog No. 5-2734

DEDICATION

The editor dedicates this book to her mother, Esther Bernice Birchett, whose life inspired its message.

ACKNOWLEDGMENTS

We wish to acknowledge the outstanding contributions of publications manager and designer, Shawan Brand; copy editor, Mary C. Lewis; Transcriber, Sara Hennings and Publications Assistant, Cheryl Wilson, without whose help the book could not have come into existence. Last, but not least, we wish to thank Media Graphics Corporation and Dickinson Press.

TABLE OF CONTENTS

PREFACE

Colleen Birchett, Ph.D.

The question of why righteous people suffer has been with us for quite some time. It dates at least as far back as the Book of Job. Job was an upright man whose life was invaded by one tragedy after another. His dilemma led him into an encounter with God that changed his life. That story is not unique. It has been repeated in the lives of thousands of God's children since time immemorial.

African Americans, in particular, are familiar with variations of this story in their lives and the lives of loved ones. However, the quest for an answer to this question can become quite intense when one is in the midst of suffering which seems unfair.

This book, *How I Got Over,* explores the issue of suffering in the Christian life. While the book does not contain any "pat" answers that can be applied across situations, it does provide the opportunity to explore the issue of suffering from a number of vantage points. First of all, the book provides a chance to explore suffering in the lives of others, and to examine the ways in which they came to know the Lord in a different way during the process of dealing with it. Secondly, the book provides a chance to study sermons by outstanding ministers from around the country, based on the Books of Job and Psalms. Thirdly, the book provides the opportunity to engage in an in-depth study of issues of suffering from a biblical perspective.

It is hoped that, upon completion of this book, the reader will have studied the issue of suffering from a number of vantage points, and will have gained insights which will help him/her deal with suffering in her/his personal life. It is also hoped that the book will provide insights for ministering to others who are suffering.

Contents. The book has an introduction, and then is divided into 12 chapters. The introduction provides information about 18th and 19th century African Americans who suffered but knew the Lord in the context of that suffering. They used a variety of strategies for dealing with their situations, from rebellion to flight, all while, like Job, waiting for their "change" to come (Job 14:14).

The remainder of the book is devoted to 20th century witnesses of God's goodness. Each chapter is divided into three sections. The first section contains testimonies of 20th century African Americans who share how they "got over" during a period of suffering. The second section of each chapter contains a sermon by an outstanding African American minister. The sermons are based on the Books of Job and Psalms, and relate in some way to the content of the personal testimonies that precede them. The third section is a Bible study application.

The Bible study application section contains seven exercises. The first five exercises contain six questions each--five exploratory "discovery" questions and a sixth summary question. Each of these five exercises allows the reader to explore topics covered in the sermons in more depth, and to apply biblical principles to his/her life. The sixth exercise is a church ministry application which provides the opportunity to explore how the content of the chapter can be applied in Christian ministry within the local church. The seventh exercise is a personal application question for applying the content of the chapter to the reader's personal life.

Ways the Book Can Be Used. One way of using the book is as a private devotional guide. After studying the introduction, the reader might study one chapter each month, completing one exercise each week, dealing with one question of a given exercise, per day. In this way, the content of the book can be spread out for an entire year. The personal application sections can be used for developing a prayer list, and perhaps as topics for seeking additional counseling from professional Christian counselors.

The book can also be used for group study. It is ideal for weekday Bible studies, Sunday School electives, and as a text for adult Vacation Bible School classes. It can also be used in leadership training sessions, and for church-wide retreats. In these contexts, the main group leader (pastor, minister or lay leader) would coordinate the activities of the group. The companion leader guide contains a lesson plan for each chapter, with discussion questions and answers to the exercises contained in the student book.

90-Minute Sessions. The lesson plan is designed for a two-part, 90-minute session. The participants would be encouraged to read the introduction to the book, in preparation for the sessions. Each session is devoted to one chapter. In Part I of a session, participants examine the testimony at the beginning of a chapter. This initial discussion would require about 25 minutes. Then the overall leader would lead the participants in discussing the sermon related to the testimony in that chapter. This would require another 25 minutes. Then the leader would help the larger group to divide into five smaller groups for the Bible study application. Each smaller group would be assigned a different numbered exercise from among the first five exercises in a given chapter. (Each individual exercise contains five questions.)

A leader would be appointed for each smaller group. That leader would assign the five exploratory questions. If the small group is larger than five people, teams of participants within the small group might work on the same question, with each team having one question. After working silently on answering a given question, participants in the small group would reconvene with the small group to share their answers, and then answer, together, the sixth exercise. Then someone would be selected to give a report to the larger group.

The overall leader would then reconvene the total group of participants and allow each small group to give a report. Then the group, together, would discuss the church ministry application exercise. Participants would be encouraged to explore the personal application exercise during the week, in private devotions.

The group study session is designed so that every person can contribute something to the understanding and application of the principles covered in the chapter.

60-Minute Sessions. If only 60 minutes are available for studying a chapter, use part of the chapter as a stimulus for discussion during the group meeting itself. The other part of the chapter might be used as "homework", and/or for private devotional study.

Church-Wide Retreats and Leadership Training. If all or part of a weekend is available for studying the book, it can be explored in a number of ways. Twelve leaders would be needed, each assigned to a different chapter. Participants would be encouraged to read the entire book prior to the retreat. They might also be encouraged to select a chapter to study in depth and during the retreat's registration period enroll in a session devoted to that chapter.

In the opening session, the overall leader (pastor, minister, or lay leader) would give a presentation (or invite a special speaker), based on the Introduction, with a focus on Job 14:14. If a musician is available, the group might be interested in singing songs related to the book's general theme, particularly the Dr. Watts hymn, "I Love the Lord, He Heard My Cry."

Each session's participants would deal with one chapter, in small groups, for the entire weekend. At the end of each plenary session, participants would form smaller groups, based on the chapter they selected for study. The plenary session speakers would deal with some aspect of Job's life. Each smaller group session would study a different aspect of the chapter, and then the Bible study application section.

The retreat's final session would be devoted to small group reports. These reports, given by representatives from each small group, would involve sharing the answers to the church ministry application sections of each chapter. The local church can use these answers to make plans for the upcoming church year.

Family Devotions. Family members might want to spread the content of the book over a year, parallel to the way in which it would be used in private devotional study. One chapter would be studied per month, one exercise per week. Each family member would select a different question from the exercise to be studied during that week, and present findings to the group. The family would discuss together, the testimony and the sermon in a given chapter, the church ministry application exercise, and the personal application section. The study of the contents would not be rushed. The family would take as much time as required, to study in depth the concepts involved.

This would be especially useful during periods when the family itself is experiencing a crisis.

Summary. The book can be used in many ways. However, the main purpose is that the reader be able to explore the issue of suffering in his/her life, and gain a more intimate relationship with the Lord, in the midst of suffering. In other words, it is hoped that the reader can say, like Job:

"If a man die, shall he live again? all the days of my appointed time will I wait, till my change come" (Job 14:14, KJV).

INTRODUCTION

Colleen Birchett, Ph.D.

"I love the Lord. He heard my cry, and pitied every groan. As long as I live, when troubles rise, I'll hasten to His throne."[1] This Dr. Watts hymn is familiar in most parts of the African American community, and it reflects sentiments, both individual and collective. Have you ever tried to imagine some of the diverse settings in which African Americans have felt, expressed and acted upon sentiments behind words such as those? In other words, have you ever allowed your soul to look back and wonder how we, as a people, "got over"?

This book, *How I Got Over,* focuses primarily on the stories of witnesses who, at the time of the book, are still living. However, we have a much larger cloud of witnesses (Hebrews 12:1-2) that stretches all of the way back to the beginning of human life, along the Nile Valley and forward into the current century.[2] On one level, it really is a cloud, in that, actually we know very little about most of our ancestors who hastened to God's throne in the time of trouble. What we have are fragmented images of them which have been gathered from here and there, by researchers who pieced them together and published them in books.

Of course it is outside of the scope of this book to discuss all of these witnesses. This book includes only 12 testimonies and 12 related sermons. At one level, we can appreciate their testimonies and sermons at face value, considering them within the times in which we are currently living. However, we can gain a deeper appreciation of them and ourselves if we consider them against the backdrop of testimonies of that great cloud of witnesses that went immediately before us, in the 18th and 19th centuries.

It is the purpose of this short introduction to *How I Got Over* to preface the 20th century witnesses included in the book, with information about a few little-known African American Christians of the 18th and 19th centuries.

Our information about 18th and 19th century ancestors comes from letters, correspondence, interviews and autobiographies of African Americans who lived during that time, published by John Blassingame, in *Slave Testimony*[3], *There Is a River* by Vincent Harding,[4] *Slave Religion,* by Albert J. Raboteau,[5] *The Historical and Cultural Atlas of African Americans* by Molefi K. Asante and Mark T. Mattson,[6] and *The Negro People* by William Foster.[7]

Before discussing testimonies of individual ancestors, it would be useful to review basic facts about the times and settings in which they lived.

Chattel Slavery. During the official period of America's involvement in the slave trade (1482 - 1888), estimates of from 15 to 50 million people were forced out of Africa.[8]

Chattel slavery was brutal, dehumanizing and lethal. Many died before they ever reached American soil. They died as they were forced to march for long distances, with their ankles chained. They died as they waited in chambers near the Atlantic Ocean, for slave ships to arrive. They died chained to one another in the basements of ships, lying almost on top of one another and in human feces. Some committed suicide rather than submit to further brutality. Others conducted mutinies to take over the ships and to attempt to return to Africa. Some succeeded and returned home to Africa. Others were killed for their defiance of the slave system. Others died shortly after they reached American soil, while waiting for brutal people to come and purchase them.

Still others died while walking for miles, with their ankles chained, on their way to slave auctions. All totaled, as many as 1/3 of the people who were captured, died before they ever reached the plantations where they were to be held in involuntary servitude.[9] More than 100 small African ethnic groups disappeared from the face of history as a result of this European chattel slavery.[10]

However, this is not the entire story. These people were not passive. As troubles rose, witnesses such as the ones that we examine in this introduction never lost hope in God.

The images of these ancestors are very powerful.

"In the midst of the journey, on many ships, they made us sing and dance...The men and women often danced separately, their music supplied by a fellow captive who beat on a broken drum or played on the upturned kettle...Then late at night, after the songs were over, from the darkness of the lower decks of the *Young Hero,* and a thousand other ships, the sailors often could hear 'a howling melancholy noise, expressive of extreme anguish.'"[11]

Could these people have been uttering the familiar sentiments behind the Dr. Watts hymn quoted at the beginning? Harding, Raboteau, Asante and others have noted that Christians, Muslims, Black Jews and those who practiced ancient African religions were all found among these captured people.[12]

By the time of the first census of 1790, there were at least 750,000 Africans in the United States.[13] By 1850, the number had increased to 3,931,860, of whom only 11% (433,807) were free.[14] In many states, Blacks outnumbered whites. However, the same firepower that was used to capture them, was used to hold them in bondage.

It was a very dangerous and unstable environment for Blacks, both enslaved and free. However, the records also contain images of such ancestors, in such troubling contexts, holding onto their hope in God and continuing to approach His throne. The records do not reflect a passive spirit. In the excerpts which follow, their words have been edited into Standard English for easier reading.

Stealing Away. By the middle of the 19th century, most of the slave holding states had passed laws regulating the type of religious activity in which slaves could engage. Slaves could not "hold church" without the supervision of whites. However, one former slave, Wash Wilson, told an interviewer:

> "When the Negroes went around singing, 'Steal Away to Jesus', that meant that there was going to be a religious meeting that night. The masters didn't like the religious meetings, so naturally we would slip off at night, down in the bottom or somewhere, where we would sing and pray all night."[15]

Lucretia Alexander described a similar meeting:

> "My father would have church in dwelling houses and they had to whisper...Sometimes they would have church at his house. That would be when they would want a real meetin' with some real preachin'...They used to sing their songs in a whisper and pray in a whisper. There was a prayer-meeting from house to house once or twice--once or twice a week."[16]

In order not to be detected by slave masters and police, these ancestors devised various means of avoiding being overheard during their prayer meetings. One way was to meet in woods, gullies, ravines, and thickets (called "hush harbors").[17]

Kalvin Woods, a preacher reported another method. In the cabins, late at night, he remembered preaching, singing and praying, while his entire congregation was huddled behind wet quilts and rags. They had wet the quilts in order to keep the sound of their voices from going out into the air.

In some cabins, they used an upturned kettle to catch sound. The pot was placed in the middle of the floor and at the doorsteps, slightly propped up to keep the sound of praying and singing from traveling.[18] This was their sanctuary, the only one most of them would know within the space of their lifetimes.

Peter Randolph, an ancestor held in bondage in Prince George

County, Virginia until 1847, described one of the church meetings held in the swamps, after midnight, when the white policemen had gone to sleep:

> "Not being allowed to hold meetings on the plantation, the slaves assembled in the swamp, out of reach of the patrols. They had an understanding among themselves as to the time and place of getting together. This was often done by the first one arriving breaking boughs from the trees, and bending them in the direction of the selected spot. Arrangements were then made for conducting the exercises. They first asked each other how they felt, the state of their mind, etc....Preaching, by the brethren, then praying and singing all around, until they generally felt quite happy...

> "The slave forgets all his sufferings, except to remind others of the trials during the past week, exclaiming: 'Thank God, I shall not live here always!' Then they pass from one to another, shaking hands, and bidding each other farewell...As they separate, they sing a parting hymn of praise."[19]

Our ancestors conducted these secret prayer meetings in spite of the danger of being discovered. Moses Grandy reported that his brother-in-law Isaac, a Black preacher held in bondage, "was flogged, and his back picked for preaching at one of these types of services."[20] Gus Clark, another formerly enslaved ancestor reported that whenever his slave owner discovered them praying or singing, he would whip them. Others reported how the masters would come into the meeting and whip all of the people and drive them out of their sanctuaries in the slave cabins.[21]

Of course, in spite of legislation against religious meetings some religious meetings were approved. Even these approved gatherings were not protected from the violence of the slave owners. In one revival, a woman by the name of Nancy Merrill had just accepted Christ as her personal Saviour when a slave trader appeared in the sanctuary with Nancy's mistress and took her away, seizing and binding her in front of the entire congregation.[22]

Yet, in spite of these troubles, the historical records carry images of ancestors who continued to hope in the Lord, continued to hastened to His throne, planned strategies of resistance and escape, and continued to wait for their change to come (Job 14:14). One of the most exciting events of their lives was baptism. Isaiah Jeffries, an ancestor held in bondage, left this image of his mother's baptism:

> "When I got to be a big boy, my Mother got religion at a camp meeting at El-Bethel. She shouted and sung for three days, going all over the plantation and to neighboring ones, inviting her friends to come to see her baptized and shouting and praying for them. She went around to all of the people that she had done wrong and begged for forgiveness. She sent for them that had wronged her, and told them that she was born again and a new woman, and that she would forgive them. She wanted everyone that was not saved to go up with her. My mother took me with her to see her baptized, and I was so happy that I sang and shouted with her. All of the Negroes joined in singing."[23]

The Dismemberment of Families. The official beginning of the American slave trade was 1619.[24] It was not until 1807 that the Congress of the United States passed legislation prohibiting Americans from purchasing slaves from Africa, or participating in the Atlantic slave trade.[25] However, it did not prohibit states from breeding and selling slaves as property in domestic markets.

Beginning in 1807, our ancestors experienced a dismemberment of their families that was parallel to the dismemberment of families that had occurred on the African continent where they were originally seized. Free Blacks were often kidnapped and sold into slavery, unable to get legal representation. Mother was sold away from child--child was sold away from mother. Husband was sold away from wife, brother was sold away from sister. Some babies were even sold in infancy. All during this time Africans were smuggled into the country from Africa, the West Indies and South America, bred, and sold.[26]

From the point of view of our ancestors, the grief must have been almost unbearable. Their letters and interviews tell the story of their efforts to locate relatives whom they had little hope of ever seeing again. Many of these letters were left on the old plantations, in the collections of slave owners. No one knows if the letters were ever read by the persons to whom they were sent. They have surfaced in the archives of libraries, museums and private historical collections, and from journalists and abolitionists.

Our ancestors reacted in many ways. Some ran away and became fugitives. Others saved money to purchase their personal freedom, and tried to raise money to purchase the freedom of other family members. Others appealed to abolitionists for money to free themselves and their relatives. Others were forced to remain in their situations, keeping hope alive by writing letters to plantations where they thought their relatives might be. People in all these situations bore similarities to Job who said:

> "If a man die, shall he live again? All the days of
> my appointed time will I wait, till my change come"
> (Job 14:14, KJV).

The 18th and 19th century ancestors left this witness in their letters, and in the interviews of fugitive and (later) emancipated slaves.

Examples. Lewis Johnson is one of those witnesses. He and his wife, Emma were in slavery until Lewis was 65 and his wife was 59. After Samuel Finley, who had held him in bondage, had died, Johnson somehow raised the money to purchase himself. His wife was then miraculously freed by the heirs of Finley. However, the children of Lewis and Emma were kept in bondage.[27]

At 65 and 59 respectively, they made the voyage over the Atlantic Ocean, back to Africa on the brig *Mary Caroline Stevens,* arriving in Careysburg, Liberia on December 25, 1857. In a letter to the heirs of Finley, Johnson pleaded with them to tell his children where their father and mother were. They reported that they were living on a half acre by 30 acre plot of land, and were still holding onto hope of raising money to purchase their children.

In the midst of this difficult situation, Johnson spoke of the goodness of God:

> "Inform them that we have been very sick, but through the kindness and the mercy of a good God we have been spared until this period of time and praised be His holy name."[28]

Another witness, Phebe Brownrigg wrote a letter to her daughter, Amy, whom she did not know whether she would ever see again. Apparently this mother and daughter had already been separated once through the domestic slave trade. In her letter of September 13, 1835, Phoebe informed her daughter Amy that she expected to be sold from Edenton, North Carolina, to an owner in Alabama.

She had no idea of where she was going. She only knew that it would be somewhere along the Mississippi River. She had no opportunity to actually send the letter, because she had been constantly interrupted and rushed to prepare for her journey. Therefore, she left the letter with her granddaughter, Emily, Amy's daughter. Apparently Phoebe and Emily had some idea of where Amy was. In probably Phoebe's last letter to her daughter, she wrote:

"Farewell, my dear child. I hope the Lord will bless you and your children, and enable you to raise them and be comfortable in life, happy in death, and may we all meet around our Father's throne in heaven, never no more to part. Farewell, my dear child. From your affectionate Mother."[29]

Just one year later, on February 12, 1836, Emily, the daughter of Amy, wrote to her mother. She said that she had heard from her, through a person by the name of Eliza Little. Apparently her mother had sent her a gift, which had been opened and inspected by the slave owners. Emily announced the bad news that her husband had been sold away from her and she did not know where he was. She grieved that she had lost her mother, grandmother, grandfather and husband. Near the end of the letter, she asked her mother:

"Grandmother wanted you to send father's hymn book, that she might have something that was his."[30]

Apparently, in this troubling circumstance, the family still found time to sing hymns to God.

Abdul Rahhahman was another witness. He wrote back from Monrovia, Liberia, on May 5, 1829, to Ralph Randolph Gurley, a graduate of Yale and an agent of the American Colonization Society, which helped raise money for Africans to return to Africa. In spite of the fact that Abdul's children were still enslaved in America, and in spite of the fact that his children would hear third hand, if at all, of his whereabouts, he kept hope alive:

"You will please inform all of my friends in America that I am in the land of my forefathers; and that I shall expect my friends in America to use their influence to get my children for me, and I shall be happy if they succeed. You will please inform my children, by letter, of my arrival in the Colony.

"As soon as the rains are over, if God be with me, I shall try to bring my countrymen to the Colony and to open a trade…"[31]

Job Ben Solomon, born around 1702, son of a Fulani high priest, was another witness. He was captured by some confused Mandingos in Africa, and sold to white slave traders, in 1731. Once on American soil, he was taken to Maryland. He wrote a letter to his father in Arabic. However, the letter miraculously got into the hands of James Oglethorpe, one of the founders of the colony of Georgia. Oglethorpe translated it and helped to purchase Job and set him free. He arranged for him to get to London, England from whence he traveled to Africa. In Job Ben Solomon's letter to a former teacher, he praises God:

"I likewise acquainted them of (testified) and all with me praised God for such His providence and goodness and as a more public acknowledgment there-of, I kept from my arrival a months fast."[32]

Another witness, a husband named George Pleasant, had been sold into slavery from Virginia to Shelbyville, Tennessee. In his letter of September 6, 1833, he told his wife that he had written many letters to her but had not heard from her. He had no idea whether she was actually still at the plantation from which he had been sold away from her. In this unsettling dilemma, he still kept hope alive by continuing to write:

"I hope with God's help that I may be able to rejoice with you on the earth and in heaven let's meet. I am determined to never stop praying, not in this earth and I hope to praise God. In glory we will meet to part no more forever. So my dear wife, I hope to meet you in paradise, to praise God forever."[33]

Another witness, Thomas Sims, ran away from his owner, James Potter of Savannah, Georgia. He was arrested in Boston and returned to Potter. Then he was sold into Tennessee, where he escaped during the Civil War and went to Boston. He wrote to Theodore Parker:

"The Undersigned is a free man, and in peril, desires the prayers of the congregation that God may deliver him from the oppressor, and restore him to freedom."[34]

Jackson Whitney, another fugitive witness, ran away from owner William Riley. In a letter, Whitney described a situation in which he had been duped by Riley. Riley had promised him that if he raised $800.00, Riley would free him and his family from slavery. When Whitney raised the money, Riley changed his mind and raised the amount to $1,000. Then, before Whitney could raise the second amount, Riley attempted to sell Whitney to another plantation. Whitney ran away rather than be sold. He fled to Canada, leaving his wife and children behind, perhaps forever. In the midst of this trouble, Whitney wrote to Riley and spoke of the Lord:

"But I rejoice to say that an unseen, kind Spirit appeared for the oppressed, and bade me take up my bed and walk--the result of which is that I am victorious and you are defeated."[35]

Hezekiah Corpsman was another witness. Apparently through prayer, he and his wife were miraculously emancipated by slave owner David Griffith. At the time, Corpsman was 43 and his wife was 40. However, Corpsman's 12-year-old son was left behind, and he did not have the money to purchase him. Corpsman had faith in God. He wrote to a newspaper in New York, *The*

Journal of Commerce, asking for people who believed in freedom and justice to send him the money to purchase his son out of slavery. The letter was published December 4, 1851, in Portsmouth, Virginia. By December 27, 1851, the money had been raised. Hezekiah wrote back to the newspaper from Portsmouth, praising God:

> "I enjoy so great a blessing. While life lasts, and though in a distant land, I shall ever pray for the happiness and prosperity of my benefactors."[36]

Finally there is the Burke family. The fragmented images of Rosabella and William Burke are found in a series of letters that they wrote to their former slave owner from Monrovia, Liberia, beginning in January of 1854. Throughout the letters, they mentioned that the previous letters had been unanswered. However, they remained hopeful, mentioning the Lord in every letter. Burke and his wife seemed like a praying man and a praying woman!

Their slave owner had been none other than Colonel Robert E. Lee, commander of the southern Confederate army, who led the troops of the states which had withdrawn from the Union because they wanted slavery to continue to be legal. The Burkes' children were being held in bondage by him! However, by the grace of God, and through their prayers, Lee miraculously freed them! By various other miracles, Burke, a Christian, had been able to get the money to travel back to Africa. Writing back to members of the Lee household, the Burkes described the area of Liberia where they were living, as a place where people were actively building sanctuaries in which to worship God.

> "I am very much pleased with the little town that we are now making. It is known at present by the name of Clay Ashland. We have quite a good sort of people about us at present, and we have a lot and house upon a beautiful hill in the township, which we have named

Mount Rest. It is about 200 yards from the river, looking down in the river, and overlooking the town. Around the house, where we are making our garden, the ground is so full of white flinty rocks that it is with difficulty that we can make a garden. I have no doubt it will be a healthy spot. We have a plenty of churches--one very fine Episcopal Church, one Baptist, one Methodist and one Presbyterian..."[37]

Certainly the spirit of the Burkes and their neighbors reminds us of the spirit of the people in our own time who fled the terrorism of the South, during the first part of the 20th century, and built storefront churches in northern cities.

We have touched on only a few lives from among the great cloud of witnesses of the 18th and 19th centuries immediately preceding us. In fact, we have not presented excerpts from more well-known people considered "giants" of that time.

Some of these giants also frequented the "hush harbors" where their spirits were also ignited. On fire for righteousness, giants like Harriet Tubman escaped from the plantation and then returned to the South, rescuing at least 300 Africans and carrying them to freedom. Fredrick Douglass and Sojourner Truth escaped from slavery and became abolitionists speaking out against slavery and for women's rights to international audiences. Thousands of giants like Nat Turner and Denmark Vessey led far-reaching insurrections, setting hundreds of captives free. Andrew Bryan and Richard Allen split from established church denominations and organized their own independent Black church movement. All of these giants became a part of that great cloud of witnesses of the 19th century.[38]

They, too, left their spirit with us--the same Spirit that inspired each of the 12 20th century testimonies and 12 20th century sermons which are presented in the remainder of this book.

The 20th century witnesses which we include in *How I Got Over*, found themselves living in this century, decades after slavery had ended. Yet they continued in the struggle, in the Spirit.

We find Maime Till-Mobley, discovering that her son, Emmet has been kidnapped and murdered by white racists in Mississippi, during the height of the 20th century phase of the Civil Rights Movement. Then there is Dr. Luther Benton, who found himself in the middle of the Vietnam War, when God called him to the ministry. We find Rev. Preston Smith, having to cope with the fact that his wife has suddenly disappeared.

We find Mother Esther Birchett, trying to raise nine children, after her house has burned to the ground. We meet Michael Jones, shot down trying to rescue his cousin from gangs in Chicago. Dr. Delores Carpenter, Rev. Diana Timberlake, and Rev. Colleen Norman report of miraculous healings. Mrs. Vera Shelbon tells of a time when she had to care for as many as four sick members of her family, in the midst of which her home is broken into and robbed.

Rev. George Liggins tells of the days as an orphan, at the beginning of the 20th century, when he had no place to lay his head other than cotton fields and trains. We find Robert Rooker, testifying of how he got over debilitating drug addiction, and Ace Ware, who talks about how he got over during the Depression.

Paired with each of these testimonies are related sermons by nationally-known African American ministers, such as Elder David Birchett, Bishop Charles Blake, Dr. Delores Carpenter, Dr. David Hall, Dr. James Earl Massey, Dr. Vashti McKenzie, Dr. Frank Madison Reid, Dr. Paul Sadler, Dr. J. Alfred Smith, Dr. Carlyle Stewart, and Rev. Diana Timberlake. The sermons are followed by Bible study applications.

Examine these testimonies and sermons, and probe the principles that are illustrated by doing the Bible study applications. Then, whatever your personal situation, keep hope alive by trusting in God!

Rev. Sandra Sanford has contributed the following poem as an introduction to the study of these testimonies and sermons. She projects an image of one who looks beyond those who erroneously consider themselves the masters of this world, to God, who is the true and loving Master of us all.

GOD

God is my master
A Paragon of virtue
A Model of probity and righteousness
My Idol, Statue of deity.
As a servant, I worship Him.
I am oriented to perform as He dictates.
His commands I obey. I would never defy Him,
for He would not assign me a chore I could
not manage.
It is my duty to encourage the power of His
strength, by inspiring in depth His concepts.
I must interpret all cycles of His concepts
with sincere concern and ignite His ambitions
and motives into spiritual realities
I must induce esteem in even His menial tasks
His challenges.
I must institute patience, endurance and yet
be persevering.
My purpose is to enhance the strength of His
character and promote His sense of dignity
and righteousness.
For it is my natural essence to endorse only
traits which please Him.
It is my spiritual obligation to exemplify all
phases of His potential.
For my God is Supreme Being
Lord of Lords
King of Kings.

Rev. Sandra Sanford

CHAPTER ONE

No Time to Cry

Coping with the death of one's child can be very difficult, but when the loss results from a violent racist act, the loss can be almost unbearable. That is what Maime Till-Mobley had to sustain, during a time when the mid-20th century phase of the Civil Rights Movement gained momentum in America. However, her loss did not destroy her, but gave her spiritual energy to devote her life to educating and "saving the seed" of the next generation.

Within a broader context, her loss can be seen within the historical framework of attempted genocide, dating at least as far back as biblical times and on forward into the final years of the 20th century. In biblical times, attempted genocide often took the form of mass murders of infants. In the first half of the 20th century, primarily it took the form of murdering thousands of African American males on "trumped up charges." Today it takes the forms of drugs, gang executions, Black-on-Black homicides, and thousands of African American men waiting on death row, even though they may be innocent.

After the testimony of Maime Till-Mobley which follows, Dr. Frank Madison Reid provides strategies for "saving the seed" today in the face of the new forms that attempted genocide has taken. Dr. Reid's focus is on the family and the church.

31

I was in bed sleeping, when my cousin Willie Mae called me to tell me that my son, 14-year-old Emmett, was missing. Her son, Curtis, had called her with the news from Money, Mississippi where Emmett was on vacation.

Apparently, two white men, a Roy Bryant and his half-brother, Milam, had come to Papa Moses Wright's home (Emmett's uncle), at around 2:30 a.m. that Sunday morning and seized Emmett. Papa Moses said that Roy had demanded, "Where is that smart-talking boy from the North?" While Papa Moses tried to convince Roy that it was unnecessary to seize Emmett, Roy took him in his car and drove away.

It was August, 1955. In Mississippi at that time it was very dangerous for young Black boys. When I heard what had happened, immediately I began to call the newspapers, radio and television stations.

Within the hour, reporters from everywhere were knocking on my door. I told them the details, as I learned them. Apparently Emmett and his cousins Maurice, Simon and Wheeler had been in a grocery store the preceding day. Roy's wife, Carolyn, was in the store at the same time. People were telling many different versions of what had happened. It was very difficult to get at the truth.

One version came from Curtis, my cousin's son, whom I learned was not there at the time but had pieced together secondhand accounts. Curtis had heard from somewhere that Emmett said, "Hi, Baby" to Carolyn. However, in later years, Curtis confessed that he was not actually there, so he had not witnessed Emmett saying anything to Carolyn.

Another account came from an unidentified girl, who said that Emmett had whistled at Roy's wife. However, Emmett whistled whenever he stuttered, in order to be able to speak better. It was a habit he had learned as a young boy, from me, when I became aware of Emmett's serious stuttering problem.

Still another account came concerning an unidentified young Black boy, who did not like Emmett because of the clothes Emmett wore, and because he came from the North. This young man had made a deal with Roy, that he would tell him something, if Roy would extend him credit. He then told Roy that Bo (Emmett's nickname) had whistled at his wife. Even though Roy's wife denied it, Roy and his half-brother still decided to seize and kill Emmett for flirting with Carolyn.

It was all very frightening, but I could not give in to my fear. Papa Moses Wright told me that he was familiar with Roy Bryant. Roy was a very cruel man who had been a foreman of laborers in the cotton fields. I was learning all of this, piece by piece, while talking to reporters, and taking one phone call after another from relatives in the South.

Then, three days later, on Wednesday of that same week, the inevitable happened. They found my son's body. When we got the call, I was sitting at my mother's table. Everyone began to scream and cry. I heard people saying, "No, no, no," over and over again. Then I stopped them, and said, "There is no time to cry. We have got to act fast. There is something that we have got to do. We will never be able to cry enough tears for Emmett Till. The world will cry for Emmett Till." Then Aunt Maime said, "Call A.A. Rainer Funeral Home."

I called A.A. Rainer, the Chicago undertaker to get the body from Mississippi. However, a Black undertaker in Mississippi was afraid to send the body because of the controversy surrounding it. It was a white undertaker in Mississippi who arranged for the body to be sent. If I had waited ten more minutes, I might not have been able to get my son's body.

The body arrived in Chicago on Friday of that same week, but the sheriff in Mississippi said that the casket could not be opened. However, when the casket arrived, after the initial shock, I demanded that the casket be opened. I had to examine the body to be sure that it was my son. I had to be sure that Emmett was not still alive, hiding in Mississippi.

On the surface, the body was not identifiable. It was badly decomposed. However, I examined the hairline, body, teeth, and the ring he was wearing. At that point, I knew it was Bo.

I insisted that the body be put on display for public viewing at Robert's Temple Church of God in Christ, in Chicago. I delayed the funeral until that next Sunday. After the funeral, the body was put back on display. Between the Friday when Emmett arrived, and the following Tuesday that we buried him, more than 600,000 people walked past the coffin to view his remains.

I wanted the world to be able to see, very clearly, what had happened to my son. Some people, both Black and white, passed out at the sight of my son. *Jet* magazine carried a picture, and the story was carried by newspapers throughout the world. Reporters from all over the world attended the funeral, interviewed me, and wrote about it.

Radio preachers from throughout the country preached about the Emmett Till case. People everywhere were demanding that something be done. I received personal letters from France, Italy, England, Denmark, Sweden, and Holland. However, some of the most remarkable letters came from various parts of Africa, in various African languages. I also received hate letters from the Ku Klux Klan and from Klan sympathizers.

Roy and his half-brother Milam were eventually brought to trial in Mississippi. During the weeks leading up to the trial, I received calls from the Ku Klux Klan, warning me that if I went to the trial they would kill me or kill members of my family. I had to have a 24-hour police guard, all the way up in Chicago, Illinois. Many Chicago police officers were wearing Ku Klux Klan stickers on their bumpers at that time. Moses Wright, Curtis, and other relatives had to leave Mississippi due to death threats.

Willie Mae, Curtis's mother, was afraid to allow Curtis to go south to the trial and testify, for fear that he would be killed. However, Papa Moses Wright, myself and other witnesses did appear at the trial. One of the most dramatic moments in the trial was when Moses Wright pointed to Roy and Milam to say that they were the ones who had seized Emmett.

Of course, the two white men were never punished for what they had done. The defense attorney claimed that there was no real evidence that the body was that of Emmett Till. While justice was never brought to these two men, Emmett's death did have a purpose. It alerted the entire world to conditions for African Americans in America of that time. It was one of the many incidents of that period that fueled the Civil Rights Movement and brought it support from all corners of the world, including Africa.

Since Emmett's death, I have been quite busy. I have helped to found several churches in the Chicago area. I have married Gene Mobley, who was once Emmett's barber. He has been such a comfort to me throughout. I have founded the Emmett Till Players, a drama group which performs throughout the city and country, and I founded the Emmett Till Scholarship Foundation. I speak throughout the country on civil rights issues. I have retired from my position as an elementary school teacher in the Chicago Public Schools. Currently I am working on a Ph.D. in ministry, from the International Seminary in Orlando, Florida.

Maime Till-Mobley

SAVING THE SEED

Dr. Frank Madison Reid
Psalm 78

A few years ago, it was my joy and honor to meet the Reverend John Cherry, of Full Gospel Temple A.M.E. Zion Church, right outside of Washington, D.C. in Temple Hills, Maryland. Dr. Cherry and his wife have a powerful teaching ministry. One focus of that ministry is what Rev. Cherry calls "Save the Seed." "Save the Seed" focuses on: African American males and young people. If one is going to save the seed one certainly must save the man, because it is the man to whom God has given the seed. If one is going to save the seed one must also save the fruit of that seed, the younger generation.

More recently, when I visited a church in North Carolina, I saw a book entitled *The Battle for the Seed*. Due to what I had learned at Dr. Cherry's church, I purchased the book. The complete title gripped my soul: *The Battle for the Seed: Spiritual Strategies to Preserve Our Children,* by Dr. Patricia Morgan. As I meditated on this concept, I reflected on the fact that not only must we save the seed, we must do battle for the seed.

The Devil's Strategy Is to Destroy the Seed. If Satan can destroy the seed, he can destroy the young people. Then he can destroy an entire generation. When one destroys an entire generation, one has in effect, destroyed a people.

Perhaps that is why African American males and African American young people are on the endangered species list. Some analyze problems of African American youth and African American males sociologically and psychologically. However, if African Americans are going to win the battle for the seed, we must recognize that it is our spiritual adversary who is trying to destroy our men and children, and through our men and children, destroy our families and our people.

Everywhere one looks, there is news of the seed being destroyed. In Baltimore, a young girl came from New York to visit her family, in the projects. They found her body thrown in a trash dump. That picture is a symbol of what the devil is trying to do to an entire generation. He wants to throw them in the trash dump of violence. He wants to throw them in the trash dump of AIDS. He wants to throw them in the trash dump of unemployment and into moral and mental castration.

The devil's strategy for destroying an entire generation is not new. As one looks at the Bible one sees that the devil has always tried to destroy the seed. Recall that when Moses was born, Pharaoh sent out a decree to kill all male children. He ordered them to be thrown into the river and drowned. When that was in-effective, he ordered the Israelite midwives to kill the children before they were born.

Recall that shortly after Jesus was born, a decree was sent out from the government to destroy every child between one and three years of age. The devil understands that if one is going to destroy people, one must begin by destroying their seed. That is how one begins--by destroying a generation. However, while the devil has a strategy of destruction, the Lord has a spiritual strategy for the seed to prosper and win.

God's Strategy to Heal the Seed. In the 78th division of the Psalms, one can locate God's strategy for the healing of God's seed. He has a strategy so that God's people can win the battle for the seed. Psalm 78 demonstrates the psalmist's understanding that if a family is to be healed, the family must be willing to hear the Word of God. When a family refuses to hear God's teaching, it cannot win the battle for the seed.

The psalmist says to the people, "Open your ears to what I am saying" (78:1, LB). How sad it is that so many children know what Michael Jackson and Public Enemy are saying, but they do not know what God is saying.

The children cannot be blamed, because the first teachers of any generations are the mothers and fathers. When mothers and fathers do not listen to the Lord, the result will be a generation that refuses to pay God any attention. Who changed their diapers? Who taught them before they knew anything about Michael Jackson, Public Enemy, or other singers?

It is sad that one can attend church every Sunday but not listen to God. Perhaps some people come to participate in a Sunday fashion show. Others may come out of habit. That is why so many people come to the house of God but do not experience a blessing. One must attend church to hear the Word of the Lord. That is the main reason for coming to church.

Listen to the psalmist who says, "Open your ears to what I am saying" (78:1). The psalmist tells of lessons from history--stories passed down from former generations. The psalmist reveals what information God's people are to pass on to the generations.

Informing the Future Generation. Readers, if one is to heal one's family, one must inform the future generation of what God has done and of what God can do. The only reason that people know anything about the Lord is that some mother, father, aunt, uncle, grandmother, or grandfather took the time to tell them. They told them that the wages of sin is death, but that the gift of God is eternal life (Romans 6:23).

However, most parents tell children to get an education, so that they will have money. Today parents tell young people not to get pregnant, and not to get AIDS. That is appropriate, but it is ineffective. Unless a parent tells them about Jesus, who has made a way for them, and who can protect them, it is ineffective. Psalm 78 provides a strategy for winning the battle for the seed. That strategy has several parts.

The Purposes of God. First one must inform the future generation about the purposes of God. Every human being is born with a purpose. Our primary purpose is not to make money, or to earn a living. God has a larger purpose than that. Parents must inform young people that God's purpose for them is not sitting in prison, rotting away somewhere, or becoming a baby maker, a heart breaker, or a cradle shaker. God's purpose has nothing to do with flipping hamburgers at McDonald's.

God's purpose is for every young person to be a world changer, one who can turn the world "upside down." They have this purpose because people of African descent have a purpose. It is a purpose that can be traced back to Genesis, to the first African man and woman who were created in Africa. All races came from these two Africans.

People of African descent need to know who they are. Africans were the originators of algebra, calculus, mathematics, and the pyramids. Today God's purpose for Africans is that they be able to operate corporations as advanced as Xerox and IBM.

That is God's purpose for Africans today.

God's Promises. Parents and leaders must also tell the next generation about God's promises. In this life, one will have trials and tribulations. In this life, one will make mistakes. However, when one knows the promises of God, one can say with the psalmist, "The Lord is my light and my salvation; whom shall I fear?" (Psalm 27:1) When one knows the promises of God, one can say, with the psalmist, "The Lord is my shepherd; I shall not want" (Psalm 23:1). When one knows the promises of God, one can say with the Apostle Paul, "I can do all things through Christ who strengthens me" (Philippians 4:13).

When one knows the promises of God, one can talk about how the Lord will fight one's battles, how the Lord is a rock in a weary land, and how the Lord is a bridge over troubled waters. When one knows the promises of God, one can say with the saints of old, "He may not come when I want Him, but He's always on time." When one knows the promises of God, one can say with the psalmist, "Weeping may endure for a night, but joy comes in the morning" (Psalm 30:5).

If we are going to heal our families, first we must know and tell others about the purposes of God. Then we must know and tell others about the promises of God. Then we must know and tell others about the provisions of God.

The Provisions of God. The Lord will provide. Reader, you would not be here if the Lord did not provide. He may not allow you to wear designer clothing. He may not give you an expensive car. However, He will provide. He'll provide you with joy in the midst of sorrow. He'll provide you with healing in the midst of sickness. He'll provide you with food in a starving land. He'll be water when you are thirsty. He'll be your lawyer when you are in trouble. Think of the many ways that the Lord has provided for you.

To save the seed we must tell about the purposes of God, about the promises of God, about the provisions of God, and about the power of God!

The Power of God. Reader, neither you nor I would be here today if it had not been for the power of God. African Americans would not have survived the Middle Passage, if it had not been for the power of God. African Americans could not have survived 400 years of slavery if it had not been for the power of God. African Americans could not have dealt with Jim Crow if it had not been for the power of God.

It is the power of God that sets a person free. The power of God will free a person from alcohol. It will free a person from jail. It will free a person from evil. It will free a person from selfishness. It will free a person from a broken heart. God has the power to set us free!

Let me tell you about the source of power. Power does not come from wearing a gold watch. It does not come from wearing a gold chain. Power does not come from having a Ph.D. Power comes from having the Holy Ghost deep down within your heart.

BIBLE STUDY APPLICATION

Instructions: Dr. Reid mentioned the need for African Americans to "save the seed." He also mentioned genocide as a threat to the seed. Genocide threatened the seed at several points in Israel's history. The exercises below provide the opportunity to study how God saved the seed at several points in Israel's history. There are five exercises, with six questions each. Then there is a church ministry application exercise and a personal application exercise.

1. Genocide and the Israelites

One of the earliest recorded attempts to completely eliminate the Israelites was in the Book of Exodus.

a. Why were the sons of Jacob (Israel) once living in Egypt rather than Canaan? (Genesis 46:28; 47:1-6)

b. What happened to the Israelites while they were in Egypt? (Exodus 1:8-10)

c. Why did the Pharaoh want to kill the Israelites? (Exodus 1:8-10)

d. How did the king plan to kill the Israelites? (Exodus 1:11-16, 22)

e. In what way did God help the Israelites to save the seed? (Exodus 1:17-21; 2:1-10; 3:1-10; 12:37-39; 14:1-30)

f. SUMMARY QUESTION: Are there any parallels between what happened to the Israelites and what has happened among African Americans of the 20th century? Are there any parallels that can be drawn between the Hebrew male children of Moses's era and African American males today? What can African Americans learn from the situation of the Israelites about "saving the seed?"

2. The Case of Athaliah

During times of political unrest, genocide was a common method of eliminating one's enemies.

a. Who was Athaliah? (2 Chronicles 22:1-4)

b. At the time that Athaliah lived, in what state was what had once been the Israelite nation? (2 Chronicles 10:19; 11:1-12)

c. What attempts at genocide did Athaliah make and why? (2 Chronicles 22:1-10; 2 Kings 11:1)

d. What attempt at genocide did Jehu make and why? (2 Kings 9:1--10:17)

e. How did Athaliah's wicked people manage to save their seed? (2 Kings 11:2-15)

f. SUMMARY QUESTION: What are the differences and similarities between what was taking place among the Israelites and gang warfare taking place within African American communities today? Is there any hope? (2 Chronicles 7:14)

3. Esther's Story

Antagonism between races and ethnic groups is often at the root of attempts at genocide.

a. Why did Haman want to kill the Jews? (Esther 3:1-6)

b. Haman's father descended from Agag, an Amalekite king. What was the history of relationships between Amalekites and Jews? (Genesis 36:9-13; 25:27-34; 27:30-36, 41-45; Numbers 20:14-21)

c. How did Haman try to carry out his plot? (Esther 3:8-15)

d. Who were Mordecai and Esther? (Esther 2:1-11)

e. How did God "save the seed?"

f. SUMMARY QUESTION: What can we learn from the boldness of Esther about taking the initiative to "save the seed?"

4. The Destruction of Jerusalem and Its People

While Nebuchadnezzar did not destroy all the Jews, he weakened them to the point where they were immobilized as a people. He created a situation in which it would have been next to impossible to "save the seed."

a. By the time of Nebuchadnezzar, what had already taken place in what was once the nation of Israel? (2 Chronicles 10:1-19; 11:1-12)

b. What was the general spiritual condition of the people by the time of Nebuchadnezzar? (Jeremiah 52:1-3)

c. Why did Nebuchadnezzar come against Judah? (Jeremiah 52:3-9)

d. In what ways did Nebuchadnezzar attempt to completely destroy Israel? (Jeremiah 52:4, 6-27)

e. How did God "save the seed?" (Lamentations 5:1-22; Ezra 1:1-11; 3:1-6, 10-11)

f. SUMMARY QUESTION: What can we learn from the situation of the Israelites about God's ability to turn a bad situation around? What does it reveal about God's mercy?

5. Herod's Plot

Herod tried to make Jesus a victim of genocide.

a. Josephus, a historian writing during the first century A.D., wrote that Herod was an Idumaen king of the Edomites. What was the historic conflict between the Jews and the Edomites? (Genesis 36:9-13; 25:27-34; 27:30-36, 41-45; Numbers 20:14-21; Deuteronomy 23:7)

b. How did Herod discover that Jesus had been born? (Matthew 2:1-3)

c. Whom did Herod believe that Jesus was? (Matthew 2:4-6)

d. What was the popular understanding among the Jews of what a Messiah would do? (Luke 24:13-24) Considering this, why did Herod try to kill Jesus?

e. How did God "save the seed?" (Matthew 2:7-23)

f. SUMMARY QUESTION: What can we learn from Herod's plot about the power of God to intervene in political situations? What do we learn about His ability to turn around a bad situation?

6. CHURCH MINISTRY APPLICATION

Dr. Reid said that the African American community is threatened by genocide. Based on this chapter, is there any hope? How can the content of this chapter be used in evangelism? How does Psalm 78 apply?

7. PERSONAL APPLICATION

Are you concerned about the escalating violence in many African American neighborhoods today? Do you feel personally threatened? How might the content of this chapter apply to your situation? How does Psalm 78 apply?

CHAPTER TWO

When Evil Strikes

Nearly an entire generation of intelligent African American men was lost during the Vietnam War of the 1960s and '70s. A large percentage of those who survived it came home mentally and physically maimed--unable to cope in a society where they were once among its most promising Black men. They were relatively the small percentage of African American males who could pass the armed services examinations. They were the ones whom the military considered most mentally and physically fit for combat. That is how we lost almost an entire generation of most able African American men. Evil came, looking for them. They did not go looking for it.

Dr. Luther Benton survived the Vietnam War, and came home as a fully-functioning citizen. In his testimony, he tells how he heard the voice of the Lord while surrounded by the evil stench of death. Following his testimony is a sermon by Dr. Vashti McKenzie, who describes what we need when trouble strikes, using the life of Job as an example.

In the middle of the Vietnam War, with the stench of death all around me, the Lord called me to the ministry.

I was a young man when I joined the United States Navy on August 28, 1961. I had an adventurous spirit. Because I was the only son in my family, I really didn't have to go into the military, but I went because I wanted to see what it was about. I believed the lie that the Communists were a threat to America, and that we had to stop them before they reached this country.

I remember that, as a young man, I had compassion and a strong sense of justice. That is why I saw things the way that I saw them. It was an ugly war, but I carried compassion and a sense of justice into the service with me.

For example, I remember that one of my first stops after joining the military was the Bay of Pigs. One night a helicopter pilot crashed into the ocean. The helicopter was sinking and some Marines were strapped into it and couldn't get out. Most of the sailors with me on the flight deck just stood watching, afraid to jump into the water. After all, it was dark, the sea was choppy, and we would be facing four to five foot waves. In spite of the danger, I, along with several other sailors got into a lifeboat to go out to the helicopter. As the lifeboat was being lowered into the water, one of the straps broke.

There was no choice but to swim. However, the other sailors crawled into the boat, while I was the only one who swam over to the helicopter. I unbuckled two people, and then two more. The guys who were back on the flight deck sent out a little boat, and we used it to get back to the flight deck. Then the helicopter sank in the water. They told me that the four guys I saved would have lost their lives if I hadn't jumped in and saved them. That is the type of young man I was.

The next stop was Vietnam. I was assigned to work at the Military Provincial Hospital Assistance Team in Hoi An for one year. My stated mission was to help upgrade the medical standards of the Vietnamese. Actually, I later discovered that this hospital was an information-gathering arm of the United States

Central Intelligence Agency.

In those days, Vietnam was ugly, evil and dangerous. It seemed as though life really had no value. The stench of death was all around me, constantly. For example, one day, I saw soldiers and policemen walking down the road in a small crowd. All of a sudden, this guy just walked into the crowd and pulled the string of a hand grenade that he was wearing around his waist. Everyone in the crowd blew up! Then other hand grenades from that guy's pockets fell out and blew up. There were about six different explosions. When the dust cleared, blood and internal body parts were scattered everywhere. That was not the only time that type of thing happened.

Sometimes, small children would run up to soldiers, with hand grenades strapped to them. They would pull the string and blow up with the soldiers, killing everyone who was anywhere near them. It was very dangerous. One night some of the Viet Cong whom we were fighting, ran into the hospital where we had been working. They fired mortars on the hospital, and the people inside were blown apart.

What made matters worse is that there were evil people on both sides of the conflict. Some of these evil people were United States Navy personnel. One day I heard a commotion, and I went over to see what it was. There before me was a young Vietnamese woman standing on a little tiny stool. The stool only had three legs on it. She was surrounded by U.S. Marines and Korean military personnel. They had taken all of her clothes off and tied her hands behind her.

One of the Marines was interrogating her. The woman became upset and spit on a Korean who was in the crowd. The Korean took a flare and stuck it up between the woman's legs, into her vagina. Then he lit it. It began to burn her legs. She fell off the stool and began flopping around. They all stood there and watched her burn to death, as she screamed for help.

In the middle of all this, I yelled out, "Hey! That's ridiculous! You shouldn't be doing that." When I started to walk over to

47

her, they all grabbed me and pulled me out of the room. They would not allow me to stop them. After that, they would never do that type of thing when I was present.

It was in the middle of this bizzare theater of war, that I heard the voice of the Lord. It happened one evening when I was sitting on a bunker watching bombs being dropped in the distance. I heard the voice of the Lord, the Holy Spirit, speak through me. I knew it was the Lord. It was like no other voice. It was not the first time I had heard the voice of the Lord.

The voice wasn't audible--like what you can hear with your ears. I felt His voice in the depths of my soul. My entire body trembled.

The voice told me that He wanted me to teach His people. At first I denied it. I thought I could escape from it by going over to a bar to have some drinks. However, the voice returned about a week later, when I was down on China Beach. In the background, there was a Catholic nun at an orphanage, and I could hear children's voices. I could also hear birds singing. Then everything seemed to stop. I couldn't hear anything but God's voice. Again, He told me that He wanted me to teach His people. I told Him that perhaps I would when I got out of the Navy.

Right after this experience with the Lord, I witnessed one of the most gruesome tragedies of the war. It happened on August 27, 1967. It was about 2:00 in the morning. I woke up and people were running everywhere. Some of the Viet Cong ran into the building where I was. By God's grace, I had on a pair of sandals, rather than combat boots, so that they could not hear me walking, and I was wearing a pair of shorts, rather than an identifiable Navy uniform. I was very thin, just like one of them. By the grace of God, I ran past them and they didn't see me.

I climbed up on a bunker with another Navy man. It wasn't long before we were engaged in fire. Before then, I had never been in involved in a fire fight. I really didn't know what to do, but again, the Lord was with me.

I just began to shoot whatever moved with my M-4. Then I threw grenades from the two boxes of grenades that we had. I threw grenades and prayed. My partner was hit, and some of the enemy ran around our rear in an armored personnel carrier. My partner shot the people in the carrier to death before they could shoot us. That was another miracle. I knew that the Lord was with us.

It wasn't long before some Viet Cong came around the corner again. This time I was facing them. They unloaded a B-40 rocket. My partner and I were lifted straight up into the air. The blast blew out my partner's eardrums. For me, another miracle took place. I must have had my mouth open, because all that I lost were the fillings in my teeth. Then another miracle took place. I fell and my weapon fell. It filled with sand and jammed. However, miraculously I shook the sand out and continued firing.

I remember continuing to shoot until daybreak. I shot at anything that moved. Later, the Navy gave me a Bronze Star. I thought I should have been given a Silver one, seeing that fighting had nothing to do with my mission for being there.

I remember on the morning after the fight, I was very aware that God had saved me for a specific purpose. To protect us (seeing that we weren't really a fighting unit, but a medical one, and one that gathered information for the CIA), the Navy moved us to an Army compound.

It was not until years later, in 1975, that I became aware of the voice of the Lord again. I was back in the states by then, in Norfolk, Virginia. It came in a very unique way. A white man walked in the door and sat beside me. He was a commissioned officer in the United States Navy. He told me that God had told him something that God wanted me to do. He said, "God wants you to get started. God wants you to go to work for Him now."

That is why I went to Ebenezer Baptist Church in Portsmith and became involved with a Bible study program for youth. Then I got transferred. However, later I heard the voice of the Lord again. It was on August 1, 1981, the day I retired from the Navy. I was a chief petty officer by then. I was driving home from Jacksonville, North Carolina and was about 20 miles from Norfolk. Again, it was not a physical sound, it was a sensation. Again He told me to teach His people, and I responded to His call.

I attended the National Theological Seminary and College in Baltimore and earned a Bachelor of Arts in religion. I was licensed as a minister in the Baptist church and began teaching Bible classes at Ebenezer Baptist Church. Today, I have earned a doctorate in theology, and I am a professor of theology at Richmond Virginia Seminary. I work for the Commonwealth of Virginia as a food and milk consultant, and I travel around the country, telling the Good News about Jesus Christ.

Dr. Luther Benton, III

WHAT DO YOU NEED WHEN TROUBLE STRIKES?

Dr. Vashti McKenzie
Job 4:4

When you are feeling the pressures of life and daily circumstances become like small stones caught in your shoe, what is it that you need? When little problems are not big enough to incapacitate you, but are enough to destroy your work, distort your walk, and slow you down, what do you need? What is it that you need most when you know there is just something that you need? What do you need the most when your quiet has been disturbed and your peace is nowhere to be found? What do you need when your eyes are swollen from sleepless nights and falling tears? What do you need most, when what has to be done seems to overwhelm you?

What is it that you need the most when life experiences and

preparation pale in the face of daily new challenges? You may be trained, educated and mentored for the tasks at hand, yet all that preparation seems woefully inadequate when the hounds of hell are tracking you down. What is it that you need when your hurt is so deep that Tylenol, Excedrin, Ibuprofin and aspirin cannot erase it? What do you need when your questions outnumber the answers given? What is it that you need when your problems outnumber your possibilities?

What is it that you need right now, this very moment? Is it a raise, a balanced checkbook, employment, a house, acceptance, to belong somewhere, respect, the love of a good man or a good woman, a good night's sleep or a moment's peace? When the time is rough and the going is hard, what do you need the most?

Allow me to respond to my own questions. If you had asked me what I need, I would sing: "I need thee, oh I need thee. Every hour I need thee. Oh, bless me now my Savior, I come to thee." I would answer that I need to know that the Lord is as close as my breath and as near as the beat of my heart. I would say that I need to know the certainty of God's presence. Every now and then the way is unclear, the road is obscure and the valley of the shadow of death is deep and dark. That is when I need to know that God is right there with me, every step of the way.

If you inquired of me, I would tell you that I need to know the everlastingness of God's love. I need to know the dailyness of new mercies. I need to know that God still provides. I need to know that "by and by" God will answer my prayer. I need to know that my sins are forgiven and I am washed in the blood of the Lamb.

I need to know that I have twins that walk with me every day: goodness on my right side and mercy on my left. I need to know that my name has been changed and written in the Lamb's book of life. I need to know that there is someone who cares enough to listen to me, regardless of how early or late I call.

When the question of needs is asked in a variety of communities, the answer I receive the most is none of the aforementioned. The most common response has been this: "I need to know that someone really cares about me."

I need someone who knows my weaknesses and cares enough not to use them against me. I need someone who knows my failures and cares enough to give me another chance. I need someone who knows my strengths and is not afraid of them. I need someone who respects my personality and personhood, caring enough not to clone me unto their image. When trouble strikes, most people want to know, "Is there someone who really cares about me?"

Can you imagine Job asking the same question (is there anyone who cares)? In Job 4, we find a man who lived a life that most people would admire. Job was an entrepreneur who was trading in sheep, ox, she-asses and producing futures. He lived in a nice neighborhood. He was self-sustaining. His 7,000 sheep, 3,000 camel, 500 yoke of oxen, and 500 yoke of she-asses were assets that in modern vernacular, would be translated as money market certificates, a blue chip stock portfolio, municipal bonds, stock options, BMW, tax shelters and an IRA account. In other words, he was independently wealthy. Job was an upscale man with a "downtown" style in the land of Uz. He had 10 children: seven boys and three girls. He could afford to feed, house, and raise them. He had a reputation that others would admire and he was on the Lord's side. Job was a good man with a reputation others admired. He was God's man.

Job walked upright and avoided evil. He lived his life avoiding evil but evil did not avoid him. Job was similar to many of us today. Some people believe that only persons living outside the will of God have trouble. However, we learn from Job that a person can be good, have a good job, home and family, and still encounter evil.

Evil has your name, address and unlisted telephone number. Evil can track you down like a hound dog chasing a rabbit at supper time. Evil waits with tragedy on one side and catastrophe on the other. Evil knows when you are sleeping, knows when you are awake, knows when you've been bad or good so be good for goodness sake. Oh, you better watch out...

Imagine now, that it is Sunday morning and you are settling in your usual pew for worship. The choir is marching into place. The pastor is preparing to pray. The ushers are about to close the sanctuary doors. Suddenly, you see Satan talking to God just beyond the last pew in the back of the church.

God asks, "Where have you been?"

Satan answers, "I've been on my morning ride, seeing whom I could see and doing what I could do. I've been observing those who call upon Your name. And well, God, frankly I've been checking Your people out!"

Clearly, not only do your friends come to check you out, but your enemies will check you out as well.

God says, "Well, have you checked out My servant Job?"

Satan says, "Yes, I have. But I tell You one thing, he loves You only because things are going good right now."

Could it be possible that Satan knew how many people viewed their relationship with God in a similar manner? Some love the Lord because the Creator gave them a house, a raise, a husband or a wife. Others love God because there is the provision of tangible possessions, prestige, power and fame. Some love the Lord because their prayers are answered on time. Others love the Lord because whatever is broken is fixed; whatever is fragmented is made whole; and because their weakness is made perfect and in the Lord's strength.

What happens when things get a little rough and a little rocky? What happens when God is slow to answer or is silent? What happens when prayers are not answered the way you want? How many remain on the Lord's side?

"Just remove the hedge from around him," Satan said. "Let me mess with him a little bit. Let me see how he handles grief, unemployment and friction with his wife. Do that and see if this man of God won't curse You."

God removed the hedge of protection from around the righteous, upright man from Uz. Job lost everything that had meaning in his life. He lost the possessions he had accumulated. He lost his financial security. He lost his sons and daughters. He lost a reasonable portion of health.

The report says that in all this, Job did not sin. He did not curse God. Yet, as we move closer to the periscope, we find a different Job speaking less stoically and piously.

Job did not curse God, but he cursed his personal life. "I wish I had never been born," Job called out to God, believing that he had done no wrong. "Where are You, God? What have I done to deserve this? Is there someone who cares about me?"

Friends have a way of showing up during seasons of joy and sadness. Friends can keep you company and even keep a secret. They are there to share your ups and if they are good friends, also will share your downs.

We've all had our share of friends. We've had fair weather friends; only when you have money friends; scratch my back and I'll scratch yours friends, shopping friends, bowling friends, kiss and tell friends, little league friends, street corner and on the job friends.

Job, too, had a few friends. Three of them, Eliphaz, Bildad and Zophar rearranged their agenda to rush to the side of a troubled friend. Job, at this point, was more important than obligations and responsibilities at home.

They sat silently for seven days, listening to Job's of complaints. If Job could sing a song at this point, it might be "Nobody Knows the Trouble I've Seen" or "In the Midst of Persecution, Stand by Me..." And, what do you think Job really needed the most when..."I went to the rock to hide my face. The rock cried out, 'No hiding place.' There's no hidin' place down here."

Eliphaz spoke first having diagnosed Job's condition. He praised Job for responding to troubled people with strong support and words of encouragement. Eliphaz criticized Job, the helper of others, for being fainthearted in the face of his own trials and troubles. It is amazing how many people believe that helpers do not need help, caretakers do not need caregiving, teachers do not need teaching, preachers preaching and ministers ministering.

Eliphaz rendered his pious opinion. What Job really needed was to confess his sin before God. The theological view of this friend appears simplistic. The righteous do not suffer and the wicked do not prosper long. Therefore, Job's troubles are viewed as an outward manifestation of some committed sin.

Job's misery increased as he was now charged with hypocrisy. Think back, Eliphaz asked Job. Name a single case where a righteous man met with disaster. Instead of being a caring presence, Job's friend adds to his misery. The distress is Job's own fault and he misrepresented himself as a righteous man.

Today, we'd call this attitude blaming the victim. The rape victim is blamed for being assaulted. The unemployed are blamed for not finding a job during an economic depression. The homeless are blamed for not being able to afford the rent or mortgage. The battered spouse is blamed for being brutally attacked.

There are two different responses to suffering people in this chapter. The first is Job's response of strength, support and encouragement. The second is Eliphaz's rebuttal of chastisement and criticism.

The cornerstone of Job's formula for helping troubled people was encouraging words. We can use words that inform, rather than inflict; words that help, rather than harm; words that confirm, rather than chastise; words that touch, rather than tear down; words that are marvelous, rather than maligning and words that spread the Gospel rather than gossip.

Job's words encouraged someone to stand when s/he had stumbled, weak and tired. We need people who will stand in the balcony of our lives, applauding and cheering us forward. What we need in our season of suffering are balcony people shouting, "Go ahead, baby! You can make it! Get up again and run with it! Work with it! Hang in there! It's going to get better! It may be dark now, but joy comes in the morning!"

Sometimes we need a break from all the Mr. and Ms. Fix-its. The "I told you so" people who saw the trouble brewing like a storm cloud on the horizon. We need a break from people who cannot identify with our hurt but are quick with fault finding, blame and criticism. Is there someone who will help us reach for the truth in troubled times?

We need to encourage each other with words but also with the Word of God. The Word of God will strengthen the heart, soul and mind in crises. The Word contains the promises of God. These promises are unfailing and sure. Promises that hold out hope to the helpless; mercy in the face of judgment; unmerited grace; comfort for the lonely; healing for the sick; courage for the cowardly; power, love and a sound mind for the fearful; companionship for the rejected and God's presence in the time of trouble. It is the Word of God that increases our faith. "For faith comes by hearing and hearing by the word of God" (Romans 10:17).

Job's formula of support included teaching. Perhaps Job taught others that the Lord gives and the Lord takes away, blessed be the name of the Lord. Perhaps Job taught others to remain faithful even when your closest family members tell you to curse God and die. Perhaps he taught them that in spite of everything, wait until your change comes.

However, as you read this chapter, you may be the person who says, "I don't have anyone I can trust. I don't have someone standing in my balcony with encouraging words or enough caring to strengthen me when I am weak and tired."

Well, think again. Yes, you do. There is Someone who cares how you are doing and wants you to do better. There is Someone who is available and will never leave you nor forsake you. There is Someone who will encourage and comfort you. There is

Someone you can count on in seasons of suffering. Someone who can satisfy your longing. Someone who will hold you up when others let you down. Someone who will let you in, when others force you out.

There is Someone who will keep you company when friends and family desert you. There is Someone who will defend you before your enemies. There is Someone who will be a friend every time. His name is Jesus.

Jesus understands our stumblings and empathizes with our suffering. He knows what it feels like to be misunderstood by your friends. He knows what it feels like to suffer publicly when He has done no wrong. Jesus knew no sin but paid sin's penalty publicly so that our sins would be forgiven.

Jesus knows what it feels like when others ask you to do for yourself, what you've done for others. Job was reminded that he taught others and now his despondent behavior indicated he needed teaching. Luke tells us that at the cross some said about Jesus, "He saved others; let him save himself, if he is the Messiah whom God has chosen!" (Matthew 27:42)

Jesus was criticized and falsely accused. His standing with God was questioned, just like Job's. He, too, felt the loneliness of abandonment as He cried from the cross, "My God, my God, Why hast thou forsaken me?" (Matthew 27:46)

Jesus is the Friend who can provide when all other resources are depleted. He is the one who can sustain when all other support systems are down. He is the Friend who is very God and very man, giving "...power to faint and to them who have no might increases strength" (Isaiah 40:29).

Jesus is the Intercessor, ever intervening on our behalf. Jesus is the Reconciler, removing all barriers between us and God. Jesus is the Saviour who came to save the people from sin. Jesus is the one who answers the door when evil knocks with sin, hell, death and the grave.

"There is not a friend like the lowly Jesus! No, no one. No, not one. Jesus knows all about our struggles. He will guide till the day is done. There's not a friend like the lowly Jesus. No, not a one, no, not one."

BIBLE STUDY APPLICATION

Instructions: Rev. McKenzie mentioned that even when a person does not seek evil, evil may seek the person. However, God has always had a plan for dealing with evil and its effects. The exercises below provide the opportunity to study what the Bible says about evil and how to deal with its effects. There are five exercises, with six questions each. Then there is a church ministry application exercise and a personal application exercise.

1. When Evil Strikes

Eliphaz the Temanite could not believe that disaster could strike a righteous person (Job 4:2). However, Rev. McKenzie points out that even though a righteous person may not seek evil, evil may seek to harm that person. Evil can come in the form of a disaster, illness or famine.

a. Who is the first righteous person who encountered a disaster? (Genesis 4:1-16)

b. Who was another righteous person who encountered evil? (2 Samuel 11:1-17)

c. Who was another righteous person who encountered evil? (Ruth 1:1-5)

d. Who was another righteous person who encountered evil? (Matthew 8:14; Mark 1:29-34; Luke 4:38-41)

e. Who is yet another righteous person who encountered a disaster? (Acts 9:36-93)

f. SUMMARY QUESTION: Consider your answers to questions a-e. Can you think of any Christian today who has encountered illness or a disaster of some type? What do all these examples reflect about the comments of Eliphaz?

2. Evil's Victims

Evil people are one of the sources of disaster coming into people's lives. Throughout history, innocent people have become victims of evil people. Consider life in the time of Isaiah the prophet (around 783-705 B.C.).

a. What was one common source of evil in Isaiah's day? (Isaiah 5:8-10) What form does this type of evil take today? Who are its innocent victims?

b. What was another common source of evil in Isaiah's day? (Isaiah 5:11-12) What form does this type of evil take today? Who are its innocent victims?

c. What was another common source of evil? (5:13-15) What form does this type of evil take today? Who are its innocent victims?

d. What was another common source of evil in Isaiah's day? (5:20-23) What form does this type of evil take today? Who are its innocent victims?

e. How does God promise, ultimately, to deal with the types of evil mentioned in questions a-d? (5:15-17; Matthew 13:47-50)

f. SUMMARY QUESTION: When an innocent person becomes a victim of evil, what does that person need? See Rev. McKenzie's comments for answers.

3. The Original Source of Evil

Evil came into the world through Satan, the enemy of God. Originally it entered the world of human beings when people disobeyed God. Today, its effects are felt by the just and the unjust.

a. Who was the original source of evil? (Ezekiel 2:12-14; Isaiah 14:12-14; 3:1-19)

b. How did evil enter the realm of human beings? (Revelations 12:7-12; Genesis 3:1-24; 4:1-16)

c. In what ways are some of the effects of evil felt by the righteous and the unrighteous? (Ecclesiastes 9:12; Matthew 5:43-48)

d. In what ways do righteous and unrighteous people experience the effects of evil differently? (Proverbs 15:15-19; Philippians 4:10-13; 1:20-26)

e. In what ways do human beings allow themselves to become agents in bringing evil into the lives of others? (Proverbs 6:12-19; 21:4-10; Matthew 12:34, 35; Mark 7:14-23; Ephesians 4:20-32)

f. SUMMARY QUESTION: What should an individual do when s/he is experiencing the effects of evil? Consult Dr. McKenzie's sermon for clues.

4. Fighting Evil

Rev. McKenzie mentions a variety of feelings that result from the invasion of evil in a person's life. While some come in the form of natural disasters and cannot be avoided, other types of evil can be avoided, if one is obedient to the Lord.

a. What is one way to fight evil? (1 Timothy 6:10; Proverbs 2:6, 20)

b. What is another way to prevent oneself from becoming a victim of certain types of evil? (Matthew 15:10-20)

c. What is another way to prevent oneself from becoming a victim of certain types of evil? (Romans 12:14-21; 1 Thessalonians 5:12-15)

d. What is yet another way to prevent oneself from becoming a victim of certain types of evil? (Colossians 3:5-10)

e. Generally speaking, whom should the Christian avoid, if the Christian wants to minimize the effects of certain types of evil in his/her life? (Ephesians 4:7; 1 Timothy 3:1-2, 6-7; 2 Timothy 2:24-26)

f. SUMMARY QUESTION: Consider your answers to questions a-e. What would be some natural negative outcomes if a person does not avoid the attitudes and behaviors mentioned? What types of evil would run rampant in the church, family and community?

5. The Lord's Triumph Over Evil

God is all-powerful. Satan is not. Therefore, the Lord can help Christians to triumph over evil in their daily lives and in the future.

a. Why would the Lord be interested in rescuing His people from evil people? (2 Thessalonians 3:1-2)

b. What is one way that the Lord rescues His people from evil? (Amos 5:14-15)

c. Describe how the Lord rescues His people on a daily basis. (Hebrews 2:14-18; Psalm 23)

d. Ultimately, what will happen to Satan? (John 12:27-33; Hebrews 10:12-13)

e. How will the forces of evil finally be quieted? (1 Corinthians 15:24-26; Revelations 20:13, 10)

f. SUMMARY QUESTION: Review your answers to questions a-e. What evidence is there that regardless of the situation, God has "the upper hand"?

6. CHURCH MINISTRY APPLICATION

If you were charged with planning a 12-week Bible study based on the content of this chapter, what would be a list of the weekly topics and related Scriptures?

7. PERSONAL APPLICATION

In what ways has your personal life been affected by evil? Review the content of this chapter and determine how the Lord can and will help you.

CHAPTER THREE

Recovery and Triumph

What happens when the pastor or minister in a church is forced into divorce? Divorce can be jarring and disruptive for almost anyone. For Christians, divorce can be so unsettling that it can disturb one's faith. However, for the minister whose family serves as a role model for other African American families, divorce can be devastating and can threaten an entire life-style. In some instances, ministers facing such dilemmas have left the pulpit altogether and have backslid into destruction.

Rev. Preston Smyth was heading for destruction, following his divorce, but the inevitable was cut short by his rededication of his life to the Lord. Rev. Smyth's recovery from his loss is in many ways parallel to that of Job of the Bible. Both were sustained by faith in God. Rev. Smyth presents his testimony here. Following it is a sermon by Dr. Carlyle Fielding Stewart, discussing the power of faith in Job's life, and how that same power can sustain us in our struggles today.

I will never forget the day, five years ago, when I had to face the fact that my marriage was over. It was a day that was not unlike any other day in my life.

I had worked late that night, and I was still at my job when my wife called me. She said that she wanted her car keys. I told her that I would bring them to her later, but she said that she wanted them then. She insisted on coming to get them, and said that her girlfriend (a neighbor) would bring her there.

It was raining when she came to the job. She took the keys, gave me a kiss on the lips and walked away. I went back to my desk and started to work again. Then, around 2:00 a.m. (during the evening shift), I called my home to tell my wife that I was on my way there, but there was no answer.

Shortly afterward, I pulled into the driveway of my home and saw that my wife's car was missing. I began to wonder where my wife could be, or who could have taken her car. Then I walked to the front door, opened it, and my eyes fell on an empty room. The furniture was all gone. Nothing was left but the plants, and a letter telling me that arrangements would be made for me to see the children. Then it all hit me. She was gone!

I guess I had ignored the warning signs, which had been occurring for at least three to four years. My wife had lost interest in sex quite some time ago. In fact, when I would try to kiss her, she would pull back. She had even told me some of her reservations about our marriage. She had said that she was tired of being a minister's wife. She had reached middle age, and she had been married since she was 19 years old.

We had met and married during a period when I had abandoned the church. However, after I was married for a while, I had come back to the church and had made a fresh commitment to the Lord. The problem was that my wife had never really become a part of my ministry.

On the day, five years ago, when I had to face the reality that my marriage was over, it was not easy. I did not want to preach anymore. I became angry with God. I came out of the pulpit altogether. My emotions went on a roller coaster. I could not see the hand of God anywhere. I felt all alone, angry, bitter and filled with hatred. Most people are unable to appreciate fully the fact that a minister sometimes needs help. In fact, there are few if any support groups for African American ministers going through the difficulties of a divorce.

Over a three- to four-week period, I did not go to church. Instead, I tried to get back into drinking. I would go to the liquor store, sit around my apartment, and talk on the telephone. I had nightly "pity parties." I would talk to anyone who would listen. In that disposition, I left the church I had been attending. I also walked off my job at General Motors, where I was a senior engineer. I decided that I didn't want anything anymore. In fact, I even thought of suicide.

Miraculously, during this period, the Lord sent a few special friends, who, unlike Job's friends, actually did help me. One of those friends was Valarie Dallas. She reminded me about Paul's saying that Christians should forget the things that are behind them, and press forward (Philippians 3:14). She kept reminding me of my calling. Other friends, like Linda Beatty and Pat Johnson, reminded me of the place of forgiveness in the Christian life. They told me that I was leaving my first love.

Then I miraculously stumbled across Les Brown. At the time, he was not as well-known as he is today. He had placed an advertisement in a newspaper for a workshop that he was holding at the Veteran's Memorial Building in Detroit. He only charged $5.00 for the workshop. At the time, he only had one tape to sell. I remember standing outside of the workshop, crying and talking to him.

I remember him telling me that I had to look beyond my present circumstances and pick myself up. I had to believe in a power that was greater than myself. I began to feel so much better. I began to read the 91st Psalm. During those days, I came to realize that God was still good.

I joined a church five or six weeks later. However, it took almost two years for me to recover, and I am still recovering. Since that time, I have developed a greeting card business. Through it, the Lord has provided for me financially. I have also started a group called L.A.D.--Life After Divorce. It is an eight-step recovery process, which I teach others to follow.

I am so thankful that I reached out to the Lord during my crisis. Today, my life is happier than it ever was before.

Rev. Preston Smyth

THE TRIUMPH OF JOB

Dr. Carlyle Fielding Stewart
Job 1:1-21

Upon reading the title of this part of the chapter, one might wonder whether the author is being facetious. Anyone having the slightest acquaintance with the peril and plight of Job knows that he endured much calamity and confusion in his life. In fact, in surveying the vast expanse of his turbulent and tumultuous experiences, one would be quite hard pressed to describe his situation as anything less than tragic. The triumph of Job seems to be a mockery of terms, for there appears to be nothing victorious about his life.

Here was a man who had everything and lost it all in one fell swoop of natural disaster. Here was a man, looked upon favorably by God, having more than his share of bounteous blessings. Here was a man whose barns were full of fresh harvest, who had seemingly endless real estate--green fields and rolling hills, resounding with the hoof beats of hordes of roving livestock. Here was a man with a beautiful family and money in the bank, the object of envy of every watchful eye in the land of Uz.

66

The Scriptures say he was upstanding and upright, feared God and shunned evil, had all the trappings of success, and bore all the trademarks of the appointed and the anointed. He was a card-carrying member of the best of the blessed because he had faithfully given his heart and soul to the Lord.

Then one cold, wispy, windy high noon, as the yellow sun broke over the brown, parched terrain of a desert oasis, cosmic gales broke loose on the four corners of his house, crashing it to the earth and killing his children as they broke bread and drank wine (Job 1:18-19). High winds blew across the desert sands, but how can winds raze houses and kill families? Was this some cosmic conspiracy designed to seduce and reduce man to a worm? Was God punishing Job for some previous transgression? How could he be riding high in May and "shot down" in May? How could his children be here today and gone today? How could he have everything, then nothing on the convulsive pulse of one breathtaking moment?

Adjectives depicting Job's state are anything but triumphant! How dare we speak of this man's fate in such vainglorious and victorious terms? How dare we use the language of conquest to describe the lot and lament of this poor man Job?

Rest assured, this discourse is not an exercise in demonic cruelty. The preacher is not trying to amuse or bemuse his hearers, for despite what happened *to* Job, what happened *in* Job is far more significant. In spite of what was taken from Job and the tragedies which beset him, he somehow managed to ride the high tide of triumph and victory by holding firm to his trust in God. His was not a commercial faith wherein he praised God *because of* his blessings, or he cashed in the chips of faith in accordance with the measures of success received. I can hear Job saying the majestic words of the great poet Tennyson, "Though much is taken, much abides," and in his own words, "Though he slay me, yet will I trust in him" (Job 13:15).

"Triumphant" is the word used to describe Job's life, because he bore the scars of battle and faced the searing swords of suffering with an unshakable faith in God. He experienced the pain of losing his children, and there is no greater grief than to lose a child or children in the white heat of death. The parents who in 1993 lost their seven children in a blazing inferno in Detroit come to mind. Despite what appears as negligence on their part, I am certain that if they have one iota of humanity, their hearts are torn asunder at their irrecoverable loss. No one can explain the depths of their hurt and sorrow, the terror such a catastrophe heaps upon them.

I know that Job wailed and decried his loss. For the pain of losing is deep and abiding, especially when there is no explicable reason for it. He had done the correct things. He recited his prayers. He treated others well and accordingly kept a good relationship with God. Then the hounds of hell were unleashed, as though Job and his family were sheep for the slaughter.

I say that Job's life was triumphant, not only because of his *response* to his condition and his fate, but because of the *obstacles* he surmounted in order to claim victory. He suffered distress in the loss of his children and wealth, and he suffered from the ignorance and cynicism of three inquisitive friends. He also suffered from the devious and diabolical actions of Satan and the attempted seduction of his wife to tempt fate and undermine his relationship with God. These scenarios posed a triple indemnity to Job. He had to struggle with his spiritual opposition as well as deal with the tragedy of his personal suffering.

Job's Response to Satan's Terrorism. Job's first triumph can be seen in his response to the *terrorism* of Satan. In spite of the claims of some liberal and New Age philosophies, evil does exist and Satan is still in the business of terrorizing the beloved of God. The hostage situation of the cult in Waco, Texas, was an example of how Satan can capture the innocent, turn their lives inside out and use them as instruments of destruction.

Satan is the prince of devious and duplicitious manipulation. He masters the subtleties of evil which guise themselves as good. God was minding His own business when Satan presented a plan to denounce Job in God's eyes. Beelzebub is always seeking to defame and discredit, to undermine and disillusion the faithful.

Job was upright, but Satan approached God with a cryptic dialogue about Job's faithfulness (Job 1:6-12). If Satan in all his wisdom and ignorance would try God, he would certainly try the children of God. However, God, in His dialogue, seems to have an air of frivolity in dealing with Satan and the fate of Job. Biblical scholars who have interpreted this text have noted that God fully understood the extent of Satan's power but never seriously considered it a threat to His providence or Job's confidence in Him.

Satan and God had a conversation about Job. Satan tried to disparage Job's righteousness. God said, "Yeah, yeah, yeah, but My servant is an upright man." Satan said, "The only reason he worships You is that You are good to him. If You take all that he has he will curse You to Your face, for Job is only a man. Besides, the only reason people serve You, God, is because of Your blessings. Take their blessings away and they cease from praising and serving You. Job is no exception."

"Are you so powerful? Then try him!" says God. God knows his man. He knows that Job is faithful and can pass the test. There is no question in God's mind that Job is upright. God really knows and understands this situation despite Satan's ploys and strategies. Satan will never cause Job to curse God.

So Satan set out on his mission to compel Job to curse God, and to destroy Job from the face of the earth. His plan was essentially one of terrorism. If he could terrorize Job into cursing God, he would succeed in destroying Job's soul. In spite of God's warning not to harm Job, Satan was determined to injure and silence the man. The plot was as diabolical and explosive as the bombs that were planted under New York's World Trade Center. The purpose was to terrorize by destroying, and that was Satan's plan for Job.

However, the terrorism didn't work. With his children dead, and sores from his head to his soles, Job scraped his wounds and sat in ashes, contemplating his relationship with God. (Job 1:13-21; 2:7-10)

Satan performs acts of physical and spiritual terrorism today. His focus is on the beloved of God. Anything designed to destroy and discredit not only the individual but his or her confidence in God is an act of spiritual terrorism. Things are happening within God's people and all around them all the time. Subtleties and spiritual conspiracies are designed to wreck confidence in ourselves and in God.

One sees evidence of these afflictions in every community of the world. One sees people covered with the sores of hopelessness, despair, disappointment and doubt. Nothing discomfits the devil more than for one to sit in contemplation of the goodness and beauty of God, painstakingly removing the burdens heaped upon oneself by these various afflictions.

Reader, think about your own life. What "sores" have been afflicted on you by evil? What "sores" have you allowed to prevent you from having the right attitude and the right relationship with God? Satan's plan of terrorism did not work with Job, but some people are allowing Satan's plan to work. Job's faith in God was too strong to be weakened, too firm to be destroyed. Job triumphed over Satan's terrorism.

Job's Triumph Over Cynicism. Second, Job also triumphed over the cynicism of his wife (2:9-10). One can empathize with the anger of Job's wife over losing her children. Many people are angry with God for similar reasons. However, the cynicism of Job's wife resided in her distrust, hatred and anger at God, and in her advice that Job should curse God and die. She didn't recommend cursing God only to release anger or release the destructive effects of emotional trauma, but she recommended cursing God to die.

Like Satan's terrorism, the cynicism of Job's wife was a further spiritual and psychological obstacle placed in Job's way. Satan declared war on Job by trying to take his life. In other words, Satan's approach was homicide. Job's wife's approach was to compel his suicide. Both approaches attempted to subvert Job's relationship with God and thereby undermine God's authority and promise.

70

Reader, what about you today, are you still holding on to your integrity or are you cursing God and dying each minute of your breathing day? Just as you cannot fully rely on friends during times of critical need, you can't always rely upon the advice of spouses and close relatives in times of need. Job's experience points to the folly of the judgments of those who are closest to us. This is particularly true when their assessments are designed to exile our relationship with God. Think of the times you were given such bad advice.

Reader, what questions are your loved ones asking you as you seek to establish and hold true to your faith? Are they such questions as: Are you still holding on to your integrity? Why are you still praying and serving and worshiping God? Why are you spending so much time at church? Why do you have to be so religious, so spiritual? Are you still holding on to your faith after all that's happened to you in the church, at the church, and through the church? Why don't you just give up your membership, curse God and die? Why would you give God the time of day, especially after all your trials and tribulations? Just curse God and die! Satan's purpose is to have you "give up" so that you can experience spiritual desolation.

Job's faith was not "commercial faith". Church pews and rows are filled with people of "commercial faith". As long as things are going fine, their relationship with God is fine. As long as the blessings are flowing, their faith is flowing. As long as there is no tragedy, no calamity, no cacophony, their belief in God is firm. However, the minute that trouble stalks and tragedy tries, they follow advice such as that of Job's wife--curse God and then die a slow spiritual death.

Job's faith was not "slot machine" faith. Some people have a Las Vegas resort town approach to faith. Their entire relationship with God is predicated upon good things that God does for them. They place their prayers and hopes in the slot machines of bounteous blessings, hoping to "hit" the big payday. As long as things are fine, their belief is fine. But the moment they are confronted with a crisis, the instant they are faced with problems which try their beliefs, they relinquish and abandon their faith. They curse God and die a slow spiritual death. They abandon their integrity and cash in their "low interest" faith dividends.

However, Christians must find more effective ways of dealing with anger. After coming to terms with grief, one must transfer concerns into proactive, positive action. Job's wife had developed a cynicism which questioned whether God really existed, but the problem was much deeper. She seems to have had a very unrealistic understanding of God in the first place. In an article in *Current Trends and Thoughts* entitled "Countering Unhealthy Ideas about God," Michael Cavanaugh says that a significant percentage of problems that people bring to ministers are caused or at least attributed to unrealistic perceptions of God. Cavanaugh cites four basic unhealthy or unhelpful notions which stymie people's ability to deal with real life crises.

First, people believe that God gets revenge and punishes people according to their sins. Second, people believe that God needs them. Third, people believe that God protects them from all harm and suffering. Fourth, people believe that when trouble strikes, God is teaching them something. Perhaps the most troubling is the belief that one will be taken out of harm's way if one lives an upright and scandal-free existence. That is, as long as one lives a life above reproach, one will not experience trials and suffering, and one's life will be exempt from personal anguish.

Archibald Macleish's play, *J.B.*, is a modern commentary on the experience of Job and personal suffering. J.B. and his wife Sarah are having a conversation. Sarah is raging about why God had to take her children. J.B. awkwardly responds that God created a world with two sides. He asks her, "Shall we take the good and not the evil? We have to take chances, Sarah: Evil with good. It doesn't mean there is no good!"

The struggle is ongoing. How do we reconcile our personal calamities and suffering with our notions of God's benevolence and goodness? The problem with cynicism is that it poses questions without providing answers. It is one thing to raise questions just for the raising. It is quite another to raise questions to get meaningful answers. The cynicism of Job's wife was an obstacle he overcame and claimed the second victory.

Job's Triumph Over Criticism. The third problem was the *criticism* of his friends. They thought they were being helpful when really they made matters worse. There is nothing like getting advice from people who are unqualified spiritually to provide sound counsel. This was the case for Job. He needed comfort, when in reality he received confrontation.

Eliphaz asked Job why he didn't practice what he preached (4:1-6). Bildad, the second friend, emphasized the justice of God and suggested that if Job was suffering there must be a cause (8:1-20). Then entered Zophar, who told Job that God gives us what we deserve and things could be much worse! (11:1-6) He advised Job to repent and seek God. He warned Job that if he did not repent he would die (11:13-20). The three friends became part of the problem rather than part of the solution. Instead of receiving comfort, Job got criticism. However, Job overcame his friends' criticism by holding fast to his faith and his belief in God.

Satan's terrorism, the cynicism of Job's wife and the criticism of Job's friends, were three things over which he claimed triumph. This was equivalent to having a spiritual triple by-pass. Everywhere he turned he was confronted with the narrow perspectives of those surrounding him.

That is why Job's life can be considered triumphant. He came to terms with the death of his children and the loss of his wealth, and he confronted three maladies which threatened to undermine his relationship with God. Job had something that no one could give or take away. He had a faith not based on human circumstances or conditions.

It was not "bargain basement" faith. It was not "tit for tat" faith. It was not a faith that could be taken away by the loss of wealth, family, friends or personal integrity. It was not a faith predicated on the ill advice of friends, nor was it vulnerable to the suicidal entreaties of his wife. It was a faith that held firm through the storms! It was a faith that could move mountains! Job could claim the victory because he knew who he was and whose he was.

Job loved the Lord. It was unconditional love! It was love not conditioned by time or circumstances! Neither the *terrorism* of Satan, the *cynicism* of his wife nor the *criticism* of his friends would prevent him from holding on to God's unchanging hand. Job held on until his life was restored in greater measure than it was before his tragedies.

BIBLE STUDY APPLICATION

Instructions: Dr. Stewart mentions that Job's triumph was primarily due to his unwavering faith in God. The exercises below provide the opportunity to study the power of faith more closely. There are five exercises, with six questions each. Then there is a church ministry application exercise and a personal application exercise.

1. Ancient Faith

No doubt Job had been influenced, to a great extent, by his knowledge of the faith of his forefathers and foremothers. In Old Testament Hebrew, "faith" was expressed using words based on the root Hebrew word *'mn*. This word meant "to sustain, support, carry." In other words, it referred to an attitude toward God that remained with a person through tests and trials.

a. What attitude toward God helped the Children of Israel through their crises? (Deuteronomy 7:1-12)

b. In God's covenant with the Israelites, what would God do? What would they do? (7:1-12) How did this covenant become a basis of their faith?

c. In addition to God's covenant, on what else would their

faith be based? (7:12)

d. What role would faith play in the well-being of the Israelites? (30:1-3)

e. What were some other foundations of the faith of the Children of Israel? (Deuteronomy 4:7-10; Exodus 13:3-4)

f. SUMMARY QUESTION: Review your answers to a-e. Compare and contrast the Children of Israel with African American Christians today, with respect to: a) God's covenant today; b) the basis of faith in God; c) the foundations of our faith; d) the impact on our faith of God's interventions in our history.

2. Abraham's Faith

One of Job's ancestors was Abraham. No doubt, Job knew about him. Abraham was mentioned in the "Hebrews Faith Hall of Fame" (Hebrews 11). His faith withstood tests and trials.

a. What was the first test of Abraham's faith? How did God want him to respond? (Genesis 11:27--12:5)

b. What was another test of Abraham's faith? (Genesis 15:1-6; 1:1-15)

c. What was yet another test of Abraham's faith? (Genesis 22:1-19)

d. What was still another test of Abraham's faith? (Genesis 22:1-19)

e. In your opinion, why was Abraham included in the "Hebrews Faith Hall of Fame?" (Hebrews 11:8-12) How might his faith story have influenced Job?

f. SUMMARY QUESTION: Identify one of your ancestors, whom you either knew personally or about whom you have heard. Compare and contrast the ancestor's faith story with that of Abraham. Mention specific tests and trials, and how the person "got over." How has this person influenced your life?

3. David's Faith

David is also mentioned in the Hebrews Hall of Fame. Job may have known about him.

a. What early experiences of God formed David's faith? (1 Samuel 16:1, 10-13; 17:34-37)

b. What is one situation through which David's faith sustained him? (1 Samuel 17:41-51)

c. What role did remembrance of God's goodness play in strengthening David's faith? (1 Samuel 17:34-37, 41-51)

d. What is another situation in which David's faith played a major role? (1 Samuel 17:6-12; 19:1-2; 24:1-15)

e. In what other experiences did David's faith play an important role? (Psalm 23)

f. SUMMARY QUESTION: Pretend that you are writing an autobiography. Develop a table of contents, with a chapter title for each major episode or phase of your life. Does each title represent a time when you had faith in God, within a different situation? In what ways has your faith sustained you over time?

4. The Power of Faith

Throughout the ministry of Jesus, He emphasized the importance of faith (*pistis*) in Him. His disciples, in carrying out His work on earth, also emphasized the power of faith.

a. What does the story of the demon-possessed boy illustrate about the power of faith? (Matthew 17:14-20; Mark 9:14-29)

b. In what way can faith in God help to overcome day-to-day difficulties? (Luke 12:22-31; Matthew 6:25-34)

c. What do the stories of Aeneas and Tabitha reveal about the power of faith? (1 Corinthians 12:9; Acts 9:32-42)

d. What does the story about the crippled man illustrate about the power of faith? (Acts 14:8-18)

e. What role would faith play in the 70 disciples' carrying out

Jesus' ministry? (Luke 10:1-12)

f. SUMMARY QUESTION: Recall a person in your church who has undergone quite a bit of suffering. Compare and contrast his/her story with those mentioned in questions a-e. What role has faith in God played in that person's life?

5. The Basis of Our Faith

The death, burial and resurrection of Christ is a strong foundation for the Christian's faith today.

a. Where does faith in God begin? What does it involve? (John 3:16; 1 Thessalonians 1:9-10; Acts 20:21-22)

b. What is one foundation of the Christian faith? (1 Corinthians 15:1-11)

c. What is another foundation of our faith? (1 Thessalonians 4:13-18)

d. What is another foundation of our faith? (Romans 6:9-14)

e. What is yet another foundation of the Christian faith? (Romans 8:31-39)

f. SUMMARY QUESTION: What is the foundation of your faith in God? Upon what is it based?

6. CHURCH MINISTRY APPLICATION

Consider your church's overall program. Where, in that program, might an extended time of the sharing of faith stories (testimonies) take place? Outline your ideas and present them to your pastor.

7. PERSONAL APPLICATION

Do you have faith in God? Have you accepted Jesus Christ as your Saviour? If not, make an appointment with one of the ministers at your church to explore this in more detail. If you have made a personal commitment to the Lord, reflect on your previous experiences with the Lord. How have they strengthened your faith today?

CHAPTER FOUR

Joy Night

My mother, Esther Birchett, weathered many storms in her life. I cannot recall even one of them that could have been foreseen. After the incidents described in her testimony below, she endured triple by-pass heart surgery, struggled with kidney disease, kidney dialysis, and finally cancer. All these storms came suddenly, but she held on, until her change came.

As Elder David Birchett says in the sermon which follows Mother Birchett's testimony, my mother's "house was built on a solid rock." When the storms came, her faith did not waver. She held onto the Lord's unchanging hand in the midst of every storm. I am printing her testimony in thanksgiving to her for the gift of faith that she shared with me, her daughter, Colleen Birchett, and with her other children.

It was Monday, "Joy Night," and it was testimony time. As usual, people were standing up and testifying of God's goodness. I was one of the first persons to stand. The church became very quiet.

"I just want to give honor to Jesus today for all that He has done for me," I began. "I have so much to thank Jesus for. You know, 22 years ago before I got saved, no one would have thought that I would have been able to make it. At that time, I had a nervous condition. I had nine children and the youngest one was retarded. My husband was sick, and was in and out of the hospital.

"During this period, one day Evangelist Taylor came by the house to collect money from my son. He asked me if I was saved. He explained to me that we needed to be born again--born by the water and the Spirit. I wasn't able to make it out to the church at that time, but not long after that my son David went to Greater Grace Temple and got saved.

"During that time, my son David was called into the ministry. Then, while I was trying to take care of my little boy, the house burned down to the ground. Most of my things burned up and I had to stay with my sister until they built the house again. Right after that happened, I went to the church to hear my son David's trial sermon.

"I will never forget David's trial sermon. He preached the 23rd Psalm. By the time I left, I knew for sure that the Lord was my Shepherd. Then one day I came to church, and Bishop Ellis gave the altar call. As I came up and repented of my sins, I was baptized in Jesus' name, filled with the Holy Ghost, and spoke in tongues.

"After that, I felt a new strength. The Lord helped me to put down the cigarettes that I was smoking. He healed me of the nervous condition. Then the Lord helped me to get a job at Mt. Carmel Mercy Hospital, even though I hadn't worked since I was 18 years old. The Lord even helped me to get three promotions on my job.

"He helped me to raise all nine of my children and He helped me to pay for one house and then get another one.

"I love this church. Bishop David Ellis is not the type of pastor that just wants people to join the church. He wants their souls saved."

Mother Esther Birchett

80

THE STORMS OF LIFE

Elder David Birchett
Job 1:1-5, 13-22; 2 Chronicles 7:14

In the first chapter of the Book of Job, we meet Job, a man who is in trouble. We meet Job after he has been hit by several storms of life. You see, the storms of life are not always predictable. They don't always follow a pattern. Job could not predict the storms of trouble that came into his life.

Picture yourself when a storm is on its way. Sometimes there are warnings, but sometimes there are no warnings. Sometimes the television weather report includes warnings and watches. When you get a "watch" it means "get ready." However, when the storm does come, all a person can do is take cover, hold on and wait for the storm to cease.

Sometimes a person can work all day long, leave the job, head toward the car, and see storm clouds and sudden darkness. It can happen so quickly that a person doesn't know what is going to happen. Have you ever tried to drive through a storm? Have you ever tried to race with time in order to find shelter before a storm strikes?

Storms, storms, storms. There are so many types of storms. There are snowstorms and hail storms. There are thunderstorms and lightning storms. There are tornadoes and hurricanes and earthquakes. Many people believe that earthquakes only take place in California. However, the daily news programs show us that earthquakes can take place anywhere.

Storms Can Take Place Anywhere. A storm can take place in one area of a town while the sun is shining in another area. When you are in the midst of a storm, sometimes all you can do is wait for the storm to stop. You can't do anything to stop it. You can't do anything to cause it to ease up. All you can do is wait for the storm to stop. You can sleep through some storms, but some storms will wake you out of your sleep. Some storms can destroy an entire neighborhood. Job's sons and daughters lost their lives in one of those storms (1:18-20).

Such a storm can cause people to change their courses for days, weeks, months, and years. A person can rise in the morning hoping to accomplish certain goals for the day, but a storm can put everything on hold. A storm can turn all earthly power off.

I remember once when our church in Marion was having a revival. The preacher was preaching while thunder and lightning was taking place outside. Then the P.A. system and the lights went out. Someone ran over from a nearby apartment and told us that we had to take cover. The preaching had to stop and we had to go down into the basement. We tried to hold service down there, but we couldn't do anything until the storm ceased.

My choir was rehearsing the song, "The Storm Is Passing Over" the other night when a sister stood and said, "Oh, yes, Lord! I am sure enough in a storm." This woman was not speaking about a tornado or hurricane. This woman was speaking about another type of storm. She was speaking of what we call storms of life. A person can experience a storm of life that won't allow the person to do anything but wait on God. Sometimes these storms of life come without warning.

When you find drugs in your child's pocket or notice changes in your child's personality, or when your child tells you he doesn't want to go to school anymore, when she gives away her clothing for drugs, you and that child are in a storm. When you try to talk to your child about the drugs, but you don't know very much about the drug storm hitting our communities, you are in a storm. When you can't determine why your child is behaving like he is, oh yes, you are in a storm!

When you are trying your best to serve the Lord and give Him all that you have, and then hell breaks loose in your house, you are in a storm. You are in a storm that can be compared to the storm in which Job found himself.

There are some men reading this chapter who are trying to be strong and "macho," but think again! Many of you are in a storm. Your family is in a storm! You may have been trying to teach your children and be good role models for them, but they do just the opposite of what you have told them to do. They go to school and out into the neighborhood and bring home filthy slang and filthy lifestyles that you do not like. You say, "I'm working all week bringing my money home, paying the bills, and doing everything I know how to do, but hell is still breaking loose.

"When I try to pray, I can't pray because it seems like trouble is wrecking my mind. When I open my Bible, I can't read it because storm clouds are hanging low over my head."

That is a storm. You are in a storm! It doesn't matter where you are from or where you are, everyone has their storms.

The Storm Will Pass Over. The storm won't last always! It comes in, does its damage, and moves on, but if you can just hold out until tomorrow, if you keep the faith through the night, everything will be all right!

I remember one day, when I was a young man in Detroit, I got caught in a storm. I was going home and it started raining. I couldn't see which way to go. My brother was in front of me, but the rain was coming down so strongly that I started to turn and tried to run back. My brother caught me by the hand and said, "Come on, David. I'm going to lead the way." I said, "I can't see." He said, "That's all right, just follow me."

You know, the storms of life are like that. When you are in a storm sometimes you can't see your way out. Then suddenly there is an unseen hand that is willing to hold your hand. The Lord wants to tell you today, just keep your hand in the hand of the Man who can calm the water. Just keep your hand in the hand of this Man who can calm the sea. If you do, you will discover that Jesus is the Master of every situation. He is the Master of the storm!

Storms hit the early church. You can read about them in the Books of Corinthians and Acts. In the Book of Acts, Peter and John were in a storm. When John's brother James was killed and Peter was put in prison, their church was in a storm! (Acts 12:1-5) Whenever your pastor is in trouble, the church is in trouble.

I am so glad that I found out what to do when my church is in a storm. I don't pick up the telephone to figure out how long the storm will last. I don't try to find someone to bail me out. No, I had to learn what the Bible in 2 Chronicles 7:14 says about storms: "If my people, which are called by my name, shall humble themselves, and pray, and seek my face, and turn from their wicked ways; then will I hear from heaven, and forgive their sin, and will heal their land." Christians need to pray in the morning, at noonday and in the midnight hour. Don't leave the church. Stay there and pray! Seek God! Turn from your wicked ways! God promises to hear you from heaven. He promises to forgive your sins and heal your church!

God has already answered you! I'll give you a personal example. When I first came to my church as pastor, I decided to purchase a drum set. We didn't have a drummer at that time. I decided to walk by faith. Someone asked me why I purchased a drum without a drummer. I answered, "Well, if we get the drums, the Lord will send a drummer. Amen!"

Then one day I began to play the drums myself. I had never played drums before, and the saints could tell. But later on, the Lord blessed us with a professional drummer! He and his wife sing and his wife is now our choir director. I couldn't write this chapter if I hadn't been through a storm myself.

A storm hit my church when some thieves broke in and took the microphone and P.A. system. They even sent back threats about what they would do if we turned their names in to the police.

The Storms of Illness. I experienced yet another type of storm. It was a storm of illness. I was saved, sanctified and filled with the Holy Ghost, but sickness wracked my body. In the

84

midst of the storm I put my eyes on the Lord. Like the Psalmist David, I said, "I will lift up mine eyes unto the hills, from whence cometh my help. My help cometh from the Lord" (Psalm 121:1-2). Like Job, I said, "Go ahead and slay me. Yet will I trust all the days of my appointed time, I'm going to wait until my change comes" (Job 14:14, paraphrased).

What do you do when you are in the midst of a storm? Let a song ring in your soul! Let a Scripture ring in your soul! Memorize a Scripture like Psalm 91! Verse one says, "He that dwelleth in the secret place of the most High shall abide under the shadow of the Almighty." Recall to yourself what Jesus said about the church in the storm. He said He would build His church, and the very gates of hell would not prevail against it (Matthew 16:18). He did not say that the devil would not be trying to overthrow it. He said the devil and the gates of hell would not overthrow it.

When a Storm Strikes the People of God. The enemy will pick a fight with the Church. He will cause confusion. He really picks on people who are not armed with the whole armor of God. Read about Peter in prison (Acts 12:1-17). He had his storm. The Bible says the church got together and prayed, and the Lord brought him out! Read about Moses! Moses had his storm (Exodus 7--11). Read about Joshua! Joshua had his storm (Joshua 9--10). One thing I like about all of them is that in the midst of their storms they kept rejoicing anyway. That's what we as Christians must do! We must keep rejoicing anyway.

Always remember that the children of God are different from other children. When a child of God goes through a storm, Jesus is in it with him or her. The child of God doesn't worry because Jesus will bring him or her out. The child of God knows that all things work together for the good of them that love the Lord and are called according to His purposes (Romans 8:28).

When the church is in a storm the world may sit back and laugh, but God is still there. The church is not going down. It is on the way up.

Through the centuries the church has weathered many storms. Our forefathers have weathered many storms. We have what we have today because our forefathers and foremothers survived many storms. Our forefathers couldn't go over to the thermostat and turn the heat up. They had to go down to the coal stove and put charcoal and wood into a furnace to get heat. Sometimes they were cold but they wouldn't stop serving the Lord. They knew what it meant to be in a storm.

Jesus' disciples also knew what it meant to be in a storm (Mark 4:37; Luke 8:22-25). When Jesus got on the boat with the disciples, He knew He was in control because before He got out of the boat, He said, "Let us go across to the other side" (Luke 8:22). He was so confident that as the boat sailed, He went to sleep.

Then a fierce wind and waves began to rock the boat. Imagine how upset the disciples were. Storms can cause us to fear if we are not careful. Finally, one of them remembered that Jesus was on board. When they awakened Jesus, He got up and rebuked the winds and waves, and they obeyed His voice! (v. 24) Then there was a great calm. You see, when you've got Jesus on board, everything is all right. But you must have Jesus on board!

Bringing Jesus on Board. How do you bring Jesus on board? Jesus can carry you in His bosom, you know. He can "pick you up" and put His arms around you and say, "You're safe, My child." Remember that David said, "Yea, though I walk through the valley of the shadow of death, I will fear no evil: for thou art with me" (Psalm 23:4).

If you are reading this chapter and you don't know the Lord, you are in a storm. You're in a terrible storm. You are in a storm that can destroy you. You may be in a storm of sin. It can destroy you. However, the Bible says that though your sins be as scarlet, God will wash them white as snow (Isaiah 1:18). All you need to do is have faith and believe that God is all powerful, and that He can do anything but fail. Believe that God is a rewarder of them that diligently seek Him.

Next, you must repent. That is, you must change and you must turn away from your sins. Tell the Lord that you are sorry. Then be baptized and receive God's Holy Spirit! God will save your soul and you will experience peace in the midst of your storm.

It is dangerous to be out in a storm and have no place for refuge. However, you can be safe, even in a storm. God is real.

If you already know the Lord as your Saviour, but you are in a storm, pray! If you can believe God, as you read this chapter, you can know that the storm is passing over. God is allowing it to pass over! There is a lesson for you in that storm. The storm is passing over! Hallelujah! Take courage. The storm is passing over!

BIBLE STUDY APPLICATION

Instructions: Elder Birchett mentioned storms that strike the Christian's life. Sometimes these storms are predictable and sometimes they are not. However, God has hope for dealing with the storms of life. The exercises below provide the opportunity to study how God deals with the storms of life. There are five exercises, with six questions each. Then there is a church ministry application exercise and a personal application question.

1. Elijah's Storm (1 Kings 19:1-21)

Elder Birchett said that we can learn quite a bit in the midst of a storm.

a. Who was Elijah? What had he done? Why did he go to Mount Carmel? (17:1; 18:1, 7-8, 15-24, 38-40; 19:1-11)

b. What were three types of storms that Elijah was experiencing? (18:3-4, 10-14, 41-45; 19:11-12)

c. In what sense was it that God was not in Elijah's storms? In what sense was it that God was there throughout the entire experience? (19:4-13)

d. Describe how God quieted each of Elijah's three storms as

87

mentioned in question b. (19:15-21) What was the pivotal point of change for Elijah?

e. In your opinion, what did Elijah learn as a result of his storms? In what sense did God use nature to teach Elijah about himself?

f. SUMMARY QUESTION: Elder Birchett mentions how "storms" can strike a congregation. What can we learn from Elijah's experience that will help us deal with "storms" that strike our churches?

2. Ezekiel's Storm (Ezekiel 1:1--2:5)

God can call a person to a special ministry in the midst of a storm.

a. What are some of the "storms" that had taken place by the time Ezekiel began his ministry? (1 Kings 12:1-11, 16-19; 2 Kings 17:1-13; 1 Kings 14:21-22)

b. What "storm" was going to take place very shortly after Ezekiel began his ministry? (2 Chronicles 36:13-20)

c. What was another "storm" that Ezekiel was about to experience? (Ezekiel 1:28--2:7)

d. Ezekiel had a vision in which God used nature to teach him something about the "storms" that he would experience. In the vision, Ezekiel saw cherubims. Whenever cherubims appear in Scripture, who is nearby? (Exodus 25:18-22; 26:1, 31-33; 1 Kings 6:23-35)

e. In your opinion, what was God saying to Ezekiel through his vision?

f. SUMMARY QUESTION: Are there any parallels that can be drawn between Ezekiel's stormy experience and "storms" that Christians experience today?

3. Peter's Storm (Matthew 14:22-32)

Elder Birchett said that when a person is in a storm, the person needs to have the faith to hold on to Jesus.

a. What were two types of "storms" that Jesus and His disciples faced? (Matthew 14:1-9, 13-15)
b. How did Jesus calm these two storms? (Matthew 14:1-20)
c. What storms did the disciples face at sea? (14:22-25)
d. How did Jesus calm the storm at sea? (14:25-32)
e. What was Jesus aiming to teach Peter about having faith in the midst of a storm? (14:29-32)
f. SUMMARY QUESTION: Do you know of someone who is experiencing a storm of life? How can you use the story of Peter's storm to help the person?

4. Jesus Calms Another Storm (Mark 4:35-41)

Elder Birchett said that it is important to discover Jesus in the midst of a storm. Some people become completely out of control in a storm because they have not discovered Jesus, with them, in the midst of the storm.

a. What did Jesus promise the disciples before the storm began? (Mark 3:35)
b. How might other people be affected by the fact that Jesus was with the disciples in their storm? (Mark 4:36) How does this relate to "storms" today?
c. Why did the disciples call Jesus "Teacher" rather than Lord? (Mark 4:38)
d. Why were the disciples frightened, even though Jesus was with them? (Mark 4:39-41)
e. What is the evidence that the disciples didn't fully understand the divinity of Christ? (Mark 4:38, 41)
f. SUMMARY QUESTION: What does it mean to discover Jesus in a storm? How do we get to know Jesus during a storm?

5. How to Prepare for a Storm

The best way to prepare for a storm is to prepare beforehand.
a. What is the meaning of a rock, as it is used to symbolize

God? (Psalm 18:1-3; 31:1-5; 40:1-2; 71:1-5)

b. How else is a rock used to symbolize God? (Psalm 18:39-46; 27:1-5; 62:1-3)

c. What did Jesus really mean when He said to build one's house on a rock? (Matthew 7:24-25)

d. What did Jesus really mean when He said that someone built his/her house on sand? (Matthew 7:26-27)

e. In what sense is Christ a rock? (Exodus 17:6; John 4:1-15; 7:37-39; 1 Corinthians 10:1-7)

f. SUMMARY QUESTION: Consider your answers to questions a-e. What is the best way to prepare for a crisis that may suddenly strike your life?

6. CHURCH MINISTRY APPLICATION

How could your church use the content of this chapter to train people who are counseling people in crisis?

7. PERSONAL APPLICATION

Are you experiencing a "storm" in your life? How can you apply the content of this chapter in getting to know Jesus in the midst of your "storm?"

CHAPTER FIVE

That Gettin' Up Stuff

What causes a person to rise from one tragedy after another, with renewed faith in God? Disease and senseless violence took one family member after another from Michael Jones. Then he was shot down in the street, as though he were a mere animal. What caused him to rise again? Dr. David Hall says that people like Michael rise again because they have "that gettin' up stuff"--the resurrection power that God gives to His children.

Read Michael Jones' testimony. Then consider, with Dr. Hall, that "gettin' up stuff" in the life of Job, and the resurrection power that God gives to His children today.

I really can't think of anything in particular that I had done to cause tragedy to strike my life the way it did. I was going about my life, in a daily routine, and tending to my personal affairs, when suddenly a series of tragedies struck my family. Then tragedy struck my physical body, leaving me unconscious, in a hospital, with three bullets lodged in me.

Prior to the tragedies, from the time I was 16 or 17 years old, I had been attending Trinity United Church of Christ in Chicago.

Two African American men whom I admired attended that church, so I followed their examples: my uncle, Reverend Reginald Johnson and Officer James Rivers, who lived across the street from me. I went to church about once a month in those days. I was also attending Chicago State University, studying accounting.

Then my great-grandfather died. Around that same time, I applied for a job at a flower shop that my church owned, called "The Flower Place." I was hired to work as a landscaper and was then promoted to delivering floral arrangements and doing custodial work. While working there, I developed a very close relationship with Sam Allen, manager of the company. He became like a father to me. My father had died more than ten years prior to when I began working at the flower shop. Sam Allen became one of the most important African American role models in my life.

After I had worked there for three or four years, the shop went out of business. Then I was hired by the church to do custodial work. In that position, I became very close to Rev. Barbara Allen, Sam Allen's wife. She became a second mother to me.

As I learned more about the Christian life, and got to know people in the Community of Faith, I began to get closer to God. One Sunday morning, Dr. Jeremiah A. Wright, Jr., my pastor, preached the sermon, "When a Black Man Meets Jesus." I listened closely to the sermon, and I believed that God was for me, and that I had no reason to shy away from Him anymore. After joining the church, everything seemed to be going smoothly.

However, right in the middle of what seemed like a fairly stable period, a series of tragedies struck. Over a period of four to five years (1987-1991), there was a death in my family nearly every year. First my great-grandfather died. Then my mother's brother died of kidney failure, about a year later.

Then one of my cousins was killed. I will never forget the brutality of my cousin's death. He had been missing for two months. We found his decayed body in an abandoned building.

He had been shot in the head, apparently kidnapped.

Not long after that, my mother died from diabetes and kidney failure. I remember not being able to understand how God could take the most important person in my life. After the loss of my mother, my family consisted of some cousins, four sisters, three younger brothers, my grandmother, and my girlfriend. Our family was very close. Losing members of the family was very difficult for all of us.

However, as though these tragedies were not enough, yet another tragedy struck. One of my younger cousins disappeared. Of course, that reminded me of how my other cousin had been kidnapped and killed. I was not going to allow that to happen to my second cousin. When my girlfriend told me that she believed my cousin had been kidnapped, we began to look for him.

We drove around the area where they said he was kidnapped. Then we saw a van that looked like my cousin's van, parked. I got out of my car and went over to the van. A guy from inside shouted out for us to get away from the van, saying that it was his van. I confronted the guy, and he shot me three times.

I remember laying in the street for at least ten minutes, while police officers were asking me questions. I remember lying there, telling myself, "Breathe. As long as you breathe, and as long as you make it to the hospital, you will be all right."

Then I began to pray.

The next memories I have are of two ministers and my pastor holding my hand. I remember laughing to myself, once I was fully conscious, and saying, "Wow! That was like being visited by the Father, Son, and Holy Ghost! These are important people at the church. Yet they took time to visit me."

All during the time I was in the hospital, the deacons of my church visited me, and Rev. James Dawkins visited me several times each week. My family also visited me. In the hospital, I began to pray more--at least three times a day. My faith began to grow.

It took three months to recover. The Community of Faith came together and really got me through that crisis.

I am back at my job at Trinity United Church of Christ. Rev. Barbara Allen and Sam Allen continue to be like parents to me, and my pastor, Rev. Jeremiah Wright, and Rev. James Dawkins are always available when I need them. They helped me when I sustained yet another loss, the death of my uncle, Rev. Reginald Johnson, in 1993.

Today, I feel that I have a much better relationship with the Lord than I once had. I pray more. I read my Bible more, and I have a better understanding of what it means to be a member of the Community of Faith.

Michael Jones

WHEN THE RIGHTEOUS CRY

Dr. David Hall
Job 3:1-26; 38:1-41; Isaiah 40:12, 13, 51

Perhaps it was Job who wrote the Book of Job. Perhaps he wrote it after he experienced a rebirth of hope following his long period of suffering. Once a person endures a long period of suffering, the turmoil isn't easily forgotten. The pain associated with the situation may remain with the person's spirit. Perhaps it was only through thinking about it, talking about it, and writing about it, that Job could get it out of his system. Perhaps Job decided that he would write his memoirs for his posterity.

The first and third chapters of Job present contrasts in Job's life experiences. In one passage (1:18), there is the unbridled recommendation of God concerning a gentleman named Job. This gentleman lived in the land of Uz, and in God's estimation,

94

was the paragon of righteousness among humankind. In this passage, God boasts about him at a gathering of heavenly beings (1:6-12). At the gathering, Satan joins them.

Job on the "Front Line." Satan's arrival signals a change in the celebrative activities. Uneasiness fills the air. When Satan starts to boast about his ability to frustrate God's elect, God challenges Satan by placing Job "on the front line." It was decided by God that Job would have to "lift up the bloodstained banner" for which the biblical pioneers and patriarchies of yesteryear gave ever valiantly. Job's immediate plight would be that of enduring Satan's many afflictions for the sake of the God he served. With this task would come a barrage of criticism from those he loved.

Christians need to remember that they can endure afflictions because God is loving and righteous. God is love. God is a provider, and God is everything underlying all that is. If the Christian can't endure for God, for whom can the Christian endure? Job felt this strongly!

However, amidst despair, confusion, and pain, Job found himself languishing away. Something within Job spoke out and said, "The Lord gave and the Lord hath taken away; blessed be the name of the Lord" (Job 1:21). Job realized that God was the source of all that he had lost, and if God wanted to take it, God could return it. Job's attitude unsettled the devil because Satan could not move Job from "square one." That is why Satan appeared before God, wanting another chance to afflict Job (2:1-6).

God told Satan that he could do whatever he wanted to do to Job, as long as he didn't take Job's life. One could suggest that the sustaining of Job's life was grace enough from God, but God is abundant in righteousness and would never give Satan complete charge. In effect Satan said to God, "If You let me at Job, I'll make him curse You. I'll make him turn his back on You. I'll make him cry bitter tears. He'll weep in frustration and he won't want to praise You or serve You anymore" (2:4-5, paraphrased).

This was a challenge that God could not allow Satan to make

unheeded. God had confidence in Job. God realized that Job was a unique individual. He realized that Job was careful to follow God's rules regarding sacrifices, worship, and praise. God knew that Job was perfect in the sense that Job had faith. Therefore God gave Satan permission to tempt Job again.

The Character of Job. Colossians 3:12-14 could be used to paint a picture of the character of Job. There the Apostle Paul encouraged the Colossians to live up to being the elect of God; he exhorted them to be tender, kind, humble, meek, longsuffering, etc. These are also qualities found in Job. The Lord reminded Satan that Job feared God, and eschewed (hated) evil (1:8; 2:3). Some people might ask why God would turn Job over to Satan. The answer is that God knew that Job would be able to bear witness to God's creation to infinitum. Said plainly, if God needed a witness, He knew where to find one.

Whenever a Christian is crying, it is because God is allowing life to run its natural course and bring about circumstances for His purpose. God needs someone who can be a witness by going all the way, without drawing back. Going all the way with the Lord is not an easy thing. When one travels down a road of pain, it is frequently a crooked, rugged road. Life turns and twists over peaks and through valleys. If a person travels with God, that person will become tired sometimes. Sometimes the individual will feel quite alone and at risk.

Still, the calamities that we find in Job's life are not outside the scope of the Christian's reality. However, Job is a good example of what one has to do in today's world: endure criticism, endure hardship and endure heartache. Recall that when Job endured these calamities, he was not unaware that they were happening according to God's will (1:21; 2:9). Initially he may have thought that God was allowing these things to happen to him for one time only. He may have thought, "Well, I guess it's my turn now."

How often has someone concluded that s/he is experiencing life's down side and sharing the same drink of bitter waters that everyone drinks? What comes to mind is a poem written by Joseph S. Cotter, Jr. This little-known Black poet was a precocious son of a well-known father. Cotter, Jr. died of tuberculosis after his second year at Fisk University. His poem, "Supplication" demonstrates the quiet desperation of a painful life and the resignation that inevitably brings some peace among the suffering.

> I am so tired and weary,
> So tired of the endless fight,
> So weary of waiting the dawn
> And finding endless night.
>
> That I ask but rest and quiet--
> Rest for the days that are gone
> And quiet for the little space
> That I must journey on.[1]

Still, when one considers Job's life, calamities continued to occur without immediate end, and death did not become the fateful lover of his soul. He endured the loss of children, riches, and property. He also had to endure a wife who became anxious when everything seemed lost. She became upset when she beheld a once rich and powerful husband impoverished, with sores from his head to his feet, broken, ragged, frustrated, crying, full of pain, locked out and forgotten by most.

Wrong Interpretations. In the midst of all this, Job's friends decided to visit him (2:11). They found him in the middle of the floor with ashes smeared all over his body. Seeing Job with boils all over him, diseased, upset and crying, Job's three friends must have thought, "Is that Job? Perhaps we should sit with him and observe his pitiful condition."

Job's friends, Eliphaz, Bildad, and Zophar observed him for seven days and nights without saying a word. Then when his friends spoke, they revealed their incorrect assumptions, misunderstandings, and wrong interpretations of the Bible. Eliphaz told Job that God did not afflict anyone unless that person has committed sin (4:7-8). This proves wrong the old saying that "misery loves company." Who wants to hear bad news when one is down and almost gone?

This was the same attitude which Jesus encountered with His disciples as they met a blind man at a roadside (John 9:1-12). Verse two raises the question of who sinned, the blind man or his parents? The Pharisees taught that creation was subject to foreordination. That is, the blindness of the man was directly related to sins he committed or those which would have been committed in his life. Therefore, to the disciples, his blindness was divine retribution. Jesus canceled this heresy, to the dismay of the disciples and especially the Pharisees, by stating that the man's blindness was done to glorify God.

The Crisis of Uncertainty. Unlike the blind man, Job had no idea of what his suffering ultimately meant and had to wait for a change to come (Job 14:14). This uncertainty was enough to make the blameless Job cry. Most Christians can identify with the cry of Job. Job's predicament, like many predicaments today, is enough to make anyone cry. Life seems perfect when the world speaks highly of us. Life seems perfect when all one hears is praise and exaltation. However, then the perfect life suddenly appears imperfect, and the once seemingly perfect person cries because his life is somewhat devalued. That is a day when your mother may not know you. It is a day when one's friends may turn their backs. It is a day when one's friends may drop their heads and won't even focus their eyes. It is a day when those who once exalted now believe that something is wrong. It is a day that will make the perfect cry. This is not a philosophic argument. This is essentially about real tears.

Job the perfect man, cried and asked God what he thought were some pertinent questions (3:11-26). There is no sin in asking God a question. One can always raise issues with God. God doesn't find it problematic. However, one has to approach God in the correct manner. When one approaches God, one must remember who God is, the Creator, and that we are His creatures. When one approaches the Creator, one must remember in whose hands one resides. Truly, one must respect, or in the words of the Old English, "fear" God.

Why the Righteous Cry. The day in which we live is a day which will cause the perfect to cry as Job did. It is a day of the deterioration of families. People marry, decide to have families, purchase homes, and cars. They work every day, and come home to enjoy each other. God is without ceremony, pushed to the edge of the mind and generally is not focused upon. Then suddenly that perfect home is shattered. Drug addiction steals a daughter. Prison takes a son. Violence claims the life of a child. A husband becomes jealous and abusive. A wife becomes flighty and inattentive.

Communication breaks down. The emotional climate of the home is shattered. A once seemingly perfect world crashes in. Then the people involved forget about God. In other words, Satan knocks on their door. Regardless of whether God has allowed it, the very devil, Satan, seizes the opportunity to knock upon the door. It is Satan's job to destroy families.

Today, incalculable trouble comes to every facet of society. When trouble comes, the righteous often cry. They cry when voices of dissent undermine the very foundations of society, causing society to cave in upon itself. The righteous cry when they witness expanding bread lines, hungry and jobless persons, and when they see families twisted and torn because meeting basic needs becomes an impossibility. The righteous cry when families break under the strain of life itself.

Trouble Must Not Destroy. However, the Christian must remember that trouble does not need to destroy a family. Remember, hard times are not new to African Americans. God has sanctified us for such times as these. Of course, sanctification relates here to the preparedness that God grants those He

99

uniquely sets aside for His purposes. Any person who is to be established through adversity must appreciate a positional stance in sanctification.

All believers are blessed equally by God to endure despair and hardship. The Christian's life should correspond to the belief He has in God. The old saints taught that one does not go out and drink or engage in immoral activity as a reaction to difficult times. When one is sanctified he/she has something to hold, and the foundation is sure. Though one walks by faith, one must lean upon the Lord.

I personally recall my grandparents, Pastor Lewis and Mother Betty Hall. Grandfather Hall completed the third grade and had a speech impediment, but he preached the Gospel. During his tenure of ministry he either built or established eight different congregations across America. At times he had guns put to his head, and the tide of public opinion was against him because people harbored ill will toward that old sanctified preacher. Through it all, my grandparents raised 12 children and educated most of them through high school and college. Several are pastors and professional persons.

Then there was my grandfather on my mother's side. His first wife, my mother's mother, Nancy Ann McClain-Allen, died when my mom was 17 years old. Grandfather Allen was confronted with raising two teenaged daughters and a teenaged son alone. The Depression was ending and World War II was in force. Still, Grandfather continued his steady efforts and was the lead deacon in their local church. The congregation could set its clock by the movements of Deacon Thomas Eugene Allen. He was the champion of deacons. God blessed him to remarry eventually but until then he was the picture of sobriety and circumspect living. Mary Bonds became his second wife and chief support. Through it all he remained sanctified, holy and righteous. For Deacon Allen and Pastor Hall, sanctification was a positional foundation upon which they lived.

100

Another provoker of crying or lamenting is when people seek to bring another person down. The righteous cry when people bring dissension into their lives. The righteous suffer when evil people place barriers in their paths to cause them to stagger backwards.

Crying Out to God. The righteous must understand that such offenses will come. However, today the Lord is saying to the righteous, "Dry your weeping eyes. Take the hump out of your back. Straighten your shoulders. Stand on your feet and lift your hands before a loving God and say, 'Lord, Give me strength, strength to endure hard times. Give me strength to walk through the valley of the shadow of death.'" As the psalm affirms, "The righteous cry out, and the Lord hears them; he delivers them from all their troubles. The Lord is close to the brokenhearted and saves those who are crushed in spirit. A righteous man may have many troubles, but the Lord delivers him from them all" (Psalm 34:17-19, NIV).

Job's friends left Job to cry out to God, alone. However, when a child of God cries, the child of God does not cry alone. Recall that Job, while he had lost almost everyone and everything, was not alone (Job 38-40). What Job needed was a fresh picture of the wonderful God that he served. If Job could have appreciated that God was always in control, it would have made a difference.

Isaiah 40:12-14 reads as follows: "Who hath measured the waters in the hollow of his hand, and meted out heaven with the span, and comprehended the dust of the earth in a measure, and weighed the mountains in scales, and the hills in a balance? Who hath directed the spirit of the Lord, or being his counsellor hath taught him? With whom took he counsel, and who instructed him, and taught him in the path of judgment, and taught him knowledge, and showed to him the way of understanding?" These words of Isaiah relate the greatness of God! One can be confident in this God.

Waiting on God. Often when the devil is battling a Christian, all the person can do is wait. However, the Christian can remember these words: "But those who wait on the Lord shall renew their strength. They shall mount up with wings like eagles. They shall run and not be weary. They shall walk and not faint" (Isaiah 40:31).

Remember that when the righteous cry, they are waiting for the inevitable lifting. They are waiting on a word! They are waiting on a song! They are waiting on a melody! They are waiting on a friend! They are waiting on a touch of the hand. The Bible says, "Wait on the Lord:...wait, I say, on the Lord" (Psalm 27:14). Surely if the example of Job in the Scriptures, the Psalms or the teachings of Isaiah mean anything, they encourage the believer to get up from life's valleys.

The world is not going to be any better to you than it was to Jesus. The contemporary Christian must remember that the difference between Job and Christians today is that Job did not know Jesus as his Saviour. He never knew that vital link between God and His creation. However, if I were speaking to Job today I would say, "Job, you don't know about Jesus. You weren't there when they nailed Him to a cross. You never heard about Jesus' resurrection and you don't know that He laid in a cold grave three days. You don't know that early in the morning, He came out of the grave and brought new hope.

"Job, you don't know about Jesus! You don't know how He fed the hungry, how He healed the sick and opened the eyes of the blind." Job didn't know Jesus! How could he? But Job did know God! Job knew Jesus' Father, who sits high and looks low. Job knew the same God who lifted him up before the devil.

It is the same God who sent for Jesus and made Him to be our sacrifice. The Bible says: "For God so loved the world, that he gave his only begotten Son, that whosoever believeth in him should not perish, but have everlasting life. For God sent not his Son into the world to condemn the world; but that the world through him might be saved" (John 3:16-17).

If I met Job today, I would say, "Job, this Jesus of whom John so wonderfully wrote came all the way from heaven, with

102

power, glory, majesty and might."

I would say, "Job, you asked in your own words, that if a man were to die, would he live again? (Job 14:14) Job, you were wondering about the resurrection in a natural sense. Job, you were wondering about the hereafter." Job wanted to know, if he died a miserable but pious death, would God's grace bring him back.

If I were to meet Job today, I would tell him that Jesus made the improbable sure--the unknown conceivable, and the unlikely a fact. The Apostle Paul expressed to the church at Philippi that a child of God must learn to know Jesus in the power of His resurrection. The child of God has got to have that "gettin' up stuff." S/he has got to know that resurrection power which will cause a person to rise from the grave. Certainly in this life one needs the power to defeat the graves of doubt, despair, and pain. One needs to be able to get up!

I would tell Job, "Job you've got to know Him in the power of His resurrection." I would tell Job to listen to the words of Paul the apostle. In Philippians 3:10, Paul says that one needs to know Christ in the "fellowship of His suffering." This is classic; there is no victory without effort.

That "Gettin' Up Stuff." Suffering is a part of this life. You've got to be a formidable foe against the devil, even at your weakest moment. When you are weak, you have got to be yet strong. You have got to be strong when your life is almost over. You've got to get in touch with the power inside--that great energizer that will cause you to get up and run with power. It is simply that "gettin' up stuff."

One must appreciate and actualize that power, vital to being sustained in the midst of suffering. One may have a tear in one's eye, but that's all right! The Bible reveals "Weeping may endure for a night [a season], but joy comes in the morning" (Psalm 30:5). When the morning comes God will dry our weeping eyes. When the morning comes, those who have that "gettin' up stuff" will be able to stand up with new power and victory in hand.

Getting up and being healed of suffering is clearly what Job was able to do. One must understand that all persons suffer in life and holding on and being victorious is what the Christian is about. The only bottom line is how we come out of a difficult experience. Will you come out bitter, broken, ugly, upset, and angry at the world? It all begins with a mind to trust God and be resurrected from the possibilities of disaster and pain.

When you know Jesus in the power of His resurrection and in the fellowship of His sufferings, you know that at the other end is the resurrection! At the other end is the gift that Jesus promised the church! Christians, Job didn't know Him! We know His power! We know His promises! We share in His hope.

We know that when the righteous cry, they don't cry in vain and without hope. Jesus related, "I do not pray that You should take them out of the world, but that You should keep them from the evil one. They are not of the world, just as I am not of the world. Sanctify them by your truth. Your word is truth" (John 17:15-17). This prayer indicates our being kept is the will of Christ. The Christian is uniquely sanctified for this purpose and Jesus will keep the Christian always.

Finally, when Job went through his suffering, he raised a question with God that rubbed God the wrong way. God answered Job with some questions of His own: "Where were you when I put the stars in place? Where were you when I blew the wind in four directions? When I sprinkled the carpet on the ground and brought forth the grass, and the flowers, where were you? Where were you when in My magnificent mind, I made every creature and everything that inhabits the sea?" (Job 38, paraprased)

Today God may be asking this generation some additional questions. "Where were you," He might be asking, "when My Son hung on the a rugged cross and died for you? Where were you when they drove the nails into His hands? Where were you when they put a crown of thorns on His head? Where were you when He gave up the ghost? Where were you?

104

"Were you among the sinners, among the liars, among the frustrators, or among the sick, crazy, maimed, or tormented? That's where I was. I was doing all I could to destroy David Hall. That's where I was! But Jesus found me and brought me to the feet of the Cross."

Thank God for the blood! Thank God for the blood which set into motion the sanctification our spirits needed.

Someone reading this article may be crying. You may be crying out of the frustration, agony and torment of your sins, and out of the many anxieties that come with them. The Bible says that you do not need to cry that type of cry anymore. Come to Jesus! Get your mind focused on Him and get your heart right. Cross over that gulf that separates you from Him. Step over. Then look back and say, "My soul looks back and wonders, how I got over." How I got over! How did I get over? How did I escape? How did I get up? It was only through the blood of Jesus!

BIBLE STUDY APPLICATION

Instructions: Dr. Hall says that when the righteous cry, they need "that gettin' up stuff." That is, they need Resurrection power! When God answered Job, he pointed to many of nature's symbols of resurrection and renewal. God hinted of a day when believers would be able to rise from troubling circumstances--even death!--by His power.

The exercises below provide the opportunity to study some of God's questions to Job more closely. There are five exercises with six questions each. Then there is a church ministry application exercise and a personal application exercise.

1. Where were you when I made the world? (Job 38:4, 12-15, 19-20)

God called Job's attention to His creation of the world. In many ways, the very creation of the world is a symbol of resurrection power--the power of God to organize and create something new, out of chaos and disorder.

a. In what environment did God create the world? (Job 38:1-7; Genesis 1:1-2)

b. What was it that brought the world into being? (Job 3:12-15, 19-20; Hebrews 11:3; John 1:1-5)

c. In Scripture, of what is darkness a symbol? (Job 10:18-22; Isaiah 8:21-22; Ephesians 5:11)

d. When light breaks into darkness, in what sense is this a symbol of renewal? (Job 3:12-15, 19-20; Isaiah 9:2-4)

e. In what ways can the symbol of light breaking into darkness be used to explain something about Jesus? (Job 3:15; John 1:1-12)

f. SUMMARY QUESTION: When you see night turn into day, what does that tell you about God's power? In what way is it a symbol of resurrection and renewal? What does it say about that "gettin' up stuff" to which Dr. Hall refers?

2. Have you visited my storerooms? (Job 38:22)

God called Job's attention to various storms and weather conditions that were all under His control. In nature, storms bring about natural conditions necessary for the renewal of plants, animals and human beings. A storm also preceded the death, burial and resurrection of Jesus Christ.

a. For what reason might God control an unruly sea? (Job 3:11; Genesis 1:6-10) How does the sea bring about birth and renewal?

b. Why are there rainstorms and hail? (Job 38:22-27, 34-36) How do rainstorms and hail bring about birth and renewal?

c. Why does cold weather exist? (Job 37:9-10; 38:22-23, 29-30) To what does it yield? How does cold weather aid in rebirth and renewal?

d. Of what is rain a symbol? (Job 38:25-28, 34; 2 Samuel 23:2-4; Psalm 84:6-7; Ezekiel 34:25-31; Hosea 6:3) How does rain aid in bringing about renewal?

e. Of what are thunder and lightning symbols? (Job 38:25, 35; 37:1-5; Psalm 18:13-14; 29:3-9) How do thunder and lightning bring about renewal?

f. SUMMARY QUESTION: Consider your answers to questions a-e. In your opinion, why might a storm have preceded the resurrection of Christ? In what sense did that storm signal rebirth, renewal, and resurrection? (Matthew 27:45-53; Mark 15:33-41; Luke 23:44-49; John 19:28-30) What does all of that have to do with your life?

3. Have you been to the springs in the depths of the sea? (Job 38:16)

In nature, what is a source of refreshment, rebirth and renewal? Water is also frequently used as a symbol of Jesus Christ and of the work the Holy Spirit.

a. In what sense does water contribute to rebirth, renewal and hope? (Psalm 65:9-10; 1:1-3; Isaiah 35:1-7)

b. What were some specific ways that water was used in cleaning? (Exodus 29:1, 4; 30:18-21; Leviticus 6:24-25, 28)

c. In Scripture, whom is water often used to represent? (Psalm 42:1-2; John 7:37-39; John 4:7-14; Isaiah 44:1-4)

d. In Scripture, what else does water frequently represent? (Isaiah 12:1-3; 41:14-20)

e. In what way does water symbolize what takes place in spiritual cleansing? (Romans 6:3-5; Colossians 2:12-15; Galatians 3:27; Matthew 28:19; Mark 16:16; 1 Peter 3:18-22)

f. SUMMARY QUESTION: Consider your answers to questions a-e. Then consider your relationship with the Lord. Have you been to the springs of the depth of God's sea? Are you as baffled about this question as Job was? Why? Why not?

4. Do you know about Jesus' resurrection power?

Dr. Hall mentioned that Job would not have known about

Jesus, when he cried out in his pain. The Christian life would be meaningless without the story of the resurrection of Jesus Christ. His resurrection is the ultimate symbol of rebirth and renewal.

a. What did Jesus say about His own resurrection? (Matthew 16:21-28; John 2:13-22)

b. When Jesus rose from the dead, who were the witnesses? (Matthew 28:1-20; Mark 16:1-10; Luke 24:1-12; John 20:1-10)

c. What did the earliest Christians teach concerning the resurrection of Christ? (Acts 2:29-35; 4:32-33; 17:22-31)

d. For Christians, how important is the story of Jesus' resurrection? (1 Peter 1:3; Philippians 3:7-11)

e. Is death the end, for believers? Explain. (John 11:17-27; Matthew 22:23-33; 1 Corinthians 15:12-28; John 5:24-29)

f. SUMMARY QUESTION: Consider your answers to questions a-e. How could you use these passages to comfort someone who is terminally ill?

5. Do you know about that "gettin' up stuff"?

Scripture contains many examples of people who experienced a type of resurrection power in daily troubling circumstances.

a. What type of "gettin' up stuff" did the paralyzed man experience? (Luke 5:17-26)

b. What type of "gettin' up stuff" did the believers in the early church experience? (Acts 4:23-31)

c. What type of "gettin' up stuff" did Paul experience? (Acts 16:1-36)

d. When Stephen faced death, what type of "gettin' up stuff" did he experience? (Acts 7:54-60)

e. What type of "gettin' up stuff" did the people of Macedonia experience? (Acts 16:6-18)

f. SUMMARY QUESTION: Consider your answers to questions a-e. Today, how can Christians experience God's resurrection power in daily circumstances?

6. CHURCH MINISTRY APPLICATION

Are there people in your church who are terminally ill? Are there those who are grieving over the loss of a loved one? How can your church come to their assistance? What types of special programs might you develop or improve? How might the content of this chapter help?

7. PERSONAL APPLICATION

Are you feeling defeated by a personal crisis? How can the content of this chapter help you to experience that "gettin' up stuff" to which Dr. Hall refers?

CHAPTER SIX

God's Healing Power

God can heal both the body and the spirit. Dr. Delores Carpenter experienced both. With the sudden onset of cancer, she turned to God, and God healed her body and her spirit. Today she is associate professor of religious education at Howard University's School of Divinity and was Dean of Academic Affairs between 1991-1992. She is the pastor of Michigan Park Christian Church in Washington, D.C. Following is her testimony and a sermon by her entitled, "A Second Chance at Life."

I will never forget the day ten years ago when I learned that I had cancer. Like any other morning, I awakened in time to prepare my children, who were seven and twelve years old at the time, for school. My husband was in Japan, with the U.S. Navy. Once the children were off to school, I was busy with my tasks for the day when the telephone rang, and I received the results of some laboratory tests from the previous week.

I learned that I had two tumors. One was four years old and benign. The other tumor was only one year old, but it was much larger and was a malignant "invasive carcinoma."

As soon as I learned of the diagnosis, I contacted my husband, who was then a Navy chaplain. He rushed home as quickly as he could. During the hours and weeks following my diagnosis, I might have felt all alone, if I had not known that the Lord was on my side. The doctors diagnosed me as Stage 3 out of 4, based on the size of the tumor. The prognosis did not look promising. As far as the doctors were concerned, they had to prepare me for the worst scenario. We discussed quality of life issues for the terminally ill.

As I reflect back now, there were many experiences that had prepared me for that moment of crisis. No doubt, somewhere in my subconscious mind, were the memories of my mother, carrying me in her womb, to different Baptist and Pentecostal churches she attended, week after week. No doubt, my subconscious mind also carried images of my grandmother, as I sat at her feet, listening to her pray for the sick. No doubt, I still carried memories of the people at the church of my youth, laying hands on the sick and rejoicing over their healing.

My childhood memories are still vivid. At that time, our extended family lived on the edge of a segregated neighborhood that separated Townson, Maryland's Black community from its white one. When someone became ill, Blacks had to travel miles past white hospitals to Johns Hopkins Hospital's colored ward. Those were the days when I had such frequent ear infections that my family had to take me to the hospital often.

Many years later, when I received the news of cancer, I remembered those former days. No doubt, I remembered when both my immediate family and church family had always turned to the Lord for their health care, regardless of the hostile environment in which we lived.

Those and many other memories prepared me for the day when I would have to do battle with cancer--memories such as the day when I met a young man at one of Rev. A.A. Allen's miracle crusades in Philadelphia. The young man had been blind, but could now see. He had been healed by the Lord! Then there was the summer of 1966, which I spent working in Rev.

Arthur Skinner's Miracles Deliverance Ministry in New York. After completing my studies at Morgan State University, I remember Rev. Skinner had called me out of a crowd of 2,000 people. He had called me his daughter, and had told me that God's anointing was on my life.

Whereupon, he hired me to read all the letters that he got and summarize for him some of the many healings of people for whom he had prayed. I remembered those letters, as well as the images of thousands of people who packed the theater each night in Brooklyn, New York City, Newark, New Jersey, and Philadelphia, seeking a healing from the Lord.

By the late summer of 1983, when I experienced my personal health crisis, there was no doubt in my mind where I should turn for healing. I opened my Bible, and, like Job, turned to the Lord. I found the Book of Job most comforting during that time in my life. I read, "But he knoweth the way that I take: when he hath tried me, I shall come forth as gold....Even today is my complaint bitter....I would order my cause before him....and fill my mouth with arguments....Will he plead against me with his great power? No; but he would put strength in me. For God maketh my heart soft" (Job 23:10, 14, 6, 16).

It wasn't long before a network of family and friends surrounded me with love and support. Two neighbors, several women ministers, including my cousin, and others all gathered in my family room and began to cry out to the Lord. We felt the presence of the Holy Spirit in the room that night.

Calls began to come from across the country, and from as far away as Canada and Korea. It was as though "the grapevine" had sent out an emergency alert and hundreds of people were praying for me. I learned again the power that comes when people touch and agree in prayer. It meant so much to me to be surrounded by people who believed in the healing power of the Almighty God.

By the night before I was to have surgery, I was content. I was surrounded by love and a great cloud of witnesses that extended as far back as my childhood. At that time, I realized that whatever the outcome, it was well with my soul! Before I went to bed that night, I opened my Bible to 2 Corinthians 4:8: "We are troubled on every side, yet not distressed; we are perplexed, but not in despair."

My prayer, as I went into surgery was, "Lord, take my eyes off of things that the doctors can see; these things are temporary. Put my eyes on things that are enduring and eternal."

A few days after the operation, I experienced a miracle. I had decided to turn over on my right side. Then I shut my eyes. Suddenly there was an intense heat that came upon my left shoulder. At first I thought that it was a reaction to my body shifting. Then I noticed that the sensation remained and had begun to move, in very slow motion, from the top of my shoulder down to my left foot. It was then that I realized that something out of the ordinary was happening. It was then that I associated the heat with the Spirit of God.

The field of heat slowly moved from the bottom of my foot back to my left shoulder. It continued to travel back and forth.

Later, the doctor and his young resident were amazed at the change that occurred. They could locate no more evidence of cancer! The surgeon was most amazed. He said that he had done many similar operations, but mine was only the second case to have such amazing results. In most similar cases, by the time they operated, the cancer had already spread to the liver, bone and brain. However, in my case, God did not allow it.

That experience brought the words of the Apostle Paul to me: "My grace is sufficient for thee: for my strength is made perfect in weakness. Most gladly therefore will I rather glory in my infirmities, that the power of Christ may rest upon me. Therefore I take pleasure in my infirmities, in reproaches, in necessities, in persecutions, in distresses for Christ's sake: for when I am weak, then am I strong" (2 Corinthians 12:9-10).

Dr. Delores Carpenter

114

A SECOND CHANCE AT LIFE

Dr. Delores Carpenter
Job 23:10; Luke 13:10-17

This chapter was not difficult to compose because it is designed to bring hope. However, it was also difficult because it was about a controversial topic. The reality of healing can be challenged by Christians who have sincerely prayed, but have not experienced a physical healing in their lives or in the lives of loved ones.

In spite of these contradictions, I still believe in the power of God to heal. A woman who was hospitalized once said to her pastor, after they prayed, "Pastor, even if I don't get well, I still believe that God is a healer." I feel very blessed to be one of the ones who overcame and is still here to tell the story.

I realize that the blessings in my own life are not due to things that I have done. I can take no credit. Trouble rains on the just as well as on the unjust. My testimony is not a tribute to self-righteousness. It is a tribute to God. In fact, it is not really my story. It is God's story.

Throughout my battle with cancer, I was reminded of Job's struggle. Recall that, at one point, sores broke out all over Job's body (Job 2:7).

The Woman in the Synagogue. The story of my healing also reminded me of a woman in Luke 13:10-17 whom Jesus healed of an ailment. When Jesus met this woman, she was bent over with a spirit of weakness. It is important to focus on the word "Spirit," because healings are spiritual as well as physical. Recall that Jesus said it was a spirit that had crippled this woman for 18 years. The woman was bound by Satan. However, Jesus set her free.

The story of the woman is particularly significant because, in the synagogue, women were not allowed in the center, particularly within worship spaces. Usually, they remained in the

115

back within the outer courtyards. Christ not only brought her into the center, but following her healing, she praised God there. That is, Jesus liberated this woman to do what only men of her time were allowed to do. Jesus took the initiative and called her into the center.

How amazing it was that Jesus even noticed the woman. She was unobtrusive in the crowd. In doing so, Jesus confronted a system of domination which had allowed women access to God only through men (fathers, husbands, or male children). Jesus demonstrated that the only domination He supported was the domination of God. Jesus was against the oppression that caused this woman to have a weak spirit. He was against sexism, satanic domination, and the spirit of weakness that was in this woman.

In those days women were treated like animals. They were considered property in the same way that oxen were. In healing this woman, Jesus presented a new perspective on women and a new perspective on illness.

Many people thought that illness was due to sin. In telling them that Satan had bound the woman, Jesus assured them that the woman didn't cause her own illness. On the contrary, she had been overtaken by a dominating spirit of weakness which was robbing her of her humanity. To Jesus, anything that was outside the will of God was of Satan. Jesus was always at war against Satan. Jesus set the woman free from bondage to Satan.

Jesus Heals. If a person took from the Gospel all accounts where Jesus healed people or cast out demons, there would not be much narrative left. Probably one third of the record of the life of Jesus is devoted to such stories. This underscores how important healing was to Jesus. Therefore, it must be important to us.

Jesus reached out, not only to this woman who was not allowed worship space in the temple, but to lepers, tax collectors, and other victims of oppressive systems. Jesus also gave this woman a new title, one that doesn't occur anywhere else in the Bible: "Daughter of Abraham." The term "Son of Abraham" was a common biblical title.

116

In naming her "Daughter of Abraham," Jesus said to her, "You don't have to have a husband to be a special relative of God. You don't have to have a son. You don't have to have a father. You are somebody as a daughter. That is the only connection you need. You are a 'Daughter of Abraham.' With that connection you have direct kinship to God."

Allowing Jesus to Touch Your Spirit. As you meditate on the content of this chapter, consider your personal spirit of weakness. Start by naming it. That is very important. What burden has bent you all these years?

Then imagine yourself like this woman, walking down a dusty street, slipping into the back of a synagogue, unobtrusively, so that no one would shoo you away. Imagine yourself praying from your heart that God would release you from 18 years of bondage. Then without your knowing it, Jesus comes into the room. He looks over the crowd to where you are and calls you to come to Him. You come to Him. Then Jesus has a word for you. He says, "You are set free!" That announcement is for everyone reading this chapter. Whatever your situation, Jesus can set you free from your ailment.

Imagine Jesus calling you and setting you free. He lays His hands on you and tells you to straighten up. Today when He says to straighten up, He may be saying to go to the health fair, to change your diet, or to begin an exercise program. He may be saying to get out from under the depression that is binding you. Reader, straighten up! Realize that God is healing you. The healing process may continue for some time. However, God is healing your Spirit! Cooperate with God's healing. If you want to be made whole today, cooperate with the healing process of God. Let weakness be replaced with a spirit of power and strength! God has set you free!

Praise God! You have something about which to praise God. He has given you a new lease on life. Thank God for the healing power in us, among us, and in the body of Christ.

BIBLE STUDY APPLICATION

Instructions: Dr. Carpenter mentioned the "great cloud of witnesses" that provided the support that led to her personal healing. The Bible is filled with instances of people who believed in God's power to heal and brought their loved ones to Jesus for healing. The following exercises provide the opportunity to examine the role that communities and families played in the healing of loved ones. There are five exercises, with six questions each. Then there is a church ministry application question and a personal application question.

1. God Heals a Little Boy (1 Kings 17:8-24)

Dr. Carpenter mentioned the important roles of her mother and grandmother in her life. The Bible is filled with stories of mothers who were healing influences in their children's lives.

a. Who was the widow of Zarephath? (1 Kings 17:8-10, 17)

b. Who was Elijah and under what circumstances had he come to Zarephath? (1 Kings 17:1-9)

c. What was wrong with the little boy? (1 Kings 17:17)

d. What evidence is there that the widow believed in God? (1 Kings 17:9, 18, 24)

e. What role did Elijah and the widow play in the healing of the little boy? (1 Kings 17:17-24)

f. SUMMARY QUESTION: Consider your answers to a-e. Rewrite the story of Elijah, the widow and her son, placing it within the context of the 20th century. How can parents today participate in the care and healing (both preventive and curative) of their children? What role can the church play?

2. God Heals a Soldier (2 Kings 5:1-15)

Dr. Carpenter mentioned that when she was a child, she learned to believe in healing. Throughout the Bible are stories

118

of children and adults with child-like faith, who helped to bring about healing in others.

a. Who was the little girl mentioned in 2 Kings 5, and how did she become involved with Naaman, the soldier? (2 Kings 5:2-3)

b. Who was Naaman and what was his problem? (5:1)

c. Name at least six people who provided various types of support that led to Naaman's healing. (5:2, 3, 5, 7, 10, 13)

d. What indication is there that the little girl believed in the power of God? (5:3)

e. What is the evidence that the people in 2 Kings 5 believed in the power of God? (5:3, 5, 7-8, 11)

f. SUMMARY QUESTION: Consider your answers to questions a-e. If you were to rewrite this story, within a 20th century context, who might these people be? What disease might Naaman have? How might these 20th century people work together to bring about Naaman's healing? In what ways might the people work together to bring about a spiritual healing, even if a physical healing does not take place?

3. Friends Become Involved

Dr. Carpenter mentioned that when her friends heard of her illness, many of them gathered at her home for prayer. Throughout Scripture, friends and relatives play important roles in the healing processes of others.

a. What role did relatives and friends play in the healing of the blind man? (Mark 8:22-26)

b. What role did friends play in healing people with various diseases? (Luke 4:40-41)

c. What role did a father play in the healing of his daughter? (Mark 5:21-24, 35-43; Matthew 9:18-26)

d. What role did a mother play in the healing of her daughter? (Mark 7:24-30)

e. What role did a son play in the healing of his mother? (Luke 4:38-39)

f. SUMMARY QUESTION: Consider your answers to questions a-e. What role did family and friends play in bringing about healing? Can family and friends play a role in bringing about spiritual healing today? Explain how this can take place.

4. Crowds Bring the Sick to Jesus

Dr. Carpenter mentioned that at one point, it seemed as though a "grapevine" of people throughout the world were praying for her. The Bible contains stories of other crowds bringing their sick to Jesus.

a. To what trouble did crowds of people go, to intercede for the sick? (Mark 6:53-56)

b. How persistent were crowds in petitioning Jesus for the sick? (Matthew 14:34-36)

c. What role did a neighborhood play in the healing of a deaf man? (Mark 7:31-37)

d. What was one result of the healings that were witnessed by the crowds? (Luke 5:16; 9:1-6, 10-11, 37)

e. What was another result of the healings that the crowds witnessed? (Luke 19:45-48)

f. SUMMARY QUESTION: Consider your answers to questions a-e. Why is it important for large groups of people to pray for sick people among them? What are some possible results?

5. People Petition Jesus Alone

Dr. Carpenter mentioned that she spent much time alone, petitioning the Lord on her own behalf.

a. What happened to the man with the swollen arms and legs? (Luke 14:1-5)

b. What two types of healings took place with the man at the Sheep Gate? (John 5:1-9)

c. What type of healing took place for the man with the dreaded skin disease? (Matthew 8:1-9)

d. What type healing took place for the woman with the "issue of blood"? (Matthew 9:20-22)

e. What type of healing took place for the demon-possessed man? (Mark 1:21-26)

f. SUMMARY QUESTION: Consider your answers to questions a-e. How could you use these Scriptures in helping sick people who have been abandoned by relatives and friends?

6. CHURCH MINISTRY APPLICATION

Does your church have a sick visitation ministry? Suppose you are called upon to design a training program for those who visit the sick. Make a list of topics and related Scriptures for a 10-week course. In what ways can you use this chapter? Dr. Carpenter mentions that not everyone will experience a physical healing. Does that mean that people cannot be healed in other ways? How would you include that type of information in your training program?

7. PERSONAL APPLICATION

Are you, a loved one, a friend, or a neighbor facing a personal health crisis? How can you apply the contents of this chapter to that situation?

CHAPTER SEVEN

God's Invisible Hand

Data from the 1990 census reflect that only about 8.1% of African Americans are 65 years of age or older. Therefore one could easily conclude that very few African Americans can remember the Great Depression of the 1930s. Probably it is difficult for most people to visualize a time more than 60 years ago, when government agencies such as welfare and Aid to Dependent Children did not exist. It was a time when most African Americans were living far below the poverty line, and no relief was in sight.

For those who can remember, the memories are like an extended nightmare of desperation and anguish. Rev. George Liggins can remember such times. With the onset of the Great Depression, he lost both of his parents and eventually became homeless. Without a job, and without a place to rest his head, he became what society called a "hobo." He hid in cotton fields and got rides on trains, finding odd jobs wherever he could.

His testimony is printed here. Following Rev. Liggins' testimony, Dr. James Earl Massey sheds more light on how God can work through the dark circumstances of life.

I am almost 80 years old now. When I look back over my life, it now seems apparent that God had an overall design for my life. He had an overall purpose, which He has fulfilled.

I was born in Mississippi, just before the Great Depression. I accepted the Lord at the age of 10, in a revival at the Beautiful Star Baptist Church in the rural area of Moundbayou, Mississippi in the Delta. Our family went to church every Sunday.

It was a very dangerous time for African American boys and men. By the time I was 14 years old, both of my parents had died. My mother died of fibroid tumors which, at that time, they could not remove. Three years later, my father died from an injury that he had gotten as a young man, working on the railroads. His injury resulted in the deterioration of the vertebrae in his backbone.

I was left in the care of my older brothers and sisters. I recall that even then, I was a leader in my family. Whenever there were disputes, my older brothers and sisters would call me in to get my opinion.

During the thirties, in the height of the Great Depression, I left home to seek public work. In other words, I became a hobo. Work was scarce in those days. I was forced to sleep overnight in the cotton fields, sneaking spaces on freight trains and riding from one place to another, looking for work and trying to hide from the railroad detectives called "Decks." I was blessed in that, whenever I would find work, I would learn different skills, which, unknown to me at the time, the Lord would later use.

It was very dangerous. For example, one time, when I was about 14 years old, I got a ride in a truck to Lula, Mississippi's day camp. The truck stopped to get gas, and I got off the truck to get water.

Suddenly there was a big white man, cursing at me and telling me that he was going to kill me. I later learned that he was a very dangerous guy named "Blind Hand Robert." He accused me of stealing some shoes. He went to get his gun, and when he came back, another man appeared out of nowhere and told him that I was not the boy who stole his shoes.

On another day, I remember that there were quite a few hobos on the train. They were talking about how railroad detectives were all over the place. There was this particular one called Winchester Slim, who got his name from being a marksman with a Winchester gun. When I was getting ready to sneak from one train to another, a white engineer on the train that I had been on, who ordinarily wouldn't even have talked to me, warned me that Winchester Slim was on the train I was about to board. I waited and boarded the next train and avoided Winchester Slim.

Then there was another day when railroad detectives were looking for hobos on the very train that I was riding. While the trains were switching, I went to get some water. I heard someone climb up on the rail. I thought it was a friend. Then the railroad "Deck" pointed a revolver at me and shot at me twice, point blank. I could smell the gunpowder.

I fell off the train and rolled out into a field. Then I ran across the field and hid, in order to see whether I was shot. It was just by the grace of God that the railroad "Deck" missed me.

One day I decided to ride the trains to New York, after stopping off in Gary, Indiana to visit an aunt. It was around 1939. I had no money. I was traveling with other hobos. One just happened to have some money, so when we arrived in Chicago, he loaned me 35 cents to catch a bus to Gary to find my aunt.

The Lord directed me straight to her door, at 2525 Filmore Avenue. When I left my aunt's home, I went with my uncle to locate my sister. I never reached New York. Again, it was the grace of God who was preparing me for something that He wanted me to do.

It was during the height of the Depression. The only employment I could get was "hiking" coals. In that job, I put coals in people's basement bins to heat their homes. That job was uncertain also, because I did not belong to the union. It cost $25.00 to join the union. Therefore, I had to take whatever work the union people didn't want. Some days I stood in the coal yard all day, waiting for work and getting none.

Pay was low. A person in my situation could earn $6.00 to $10.00 in a good week's work. However, $6.00 was the cost of one month's rent. A person could earn 16 cents for shoveling a ton (2,000 pounds of coal), 43 cents per ton for wheeling the coal, and 51 cents per ton for putting it in bags and carrying the bags. I have made as low as 16 cents in a day and as high as $6.00 per week.

The only way we were able to make it is that my family stuck together. We lived together in one apartment. We paid for a half a ton of coal to heat the apartment, and it lasted for about one month.

Although I had been raised a Christian, I strayed away from my upbringing during those days. After I finally got some permanent employment, I got married, only to learn three months later, that I was drafted into the army.

By then, World War II was raging. Unknown to me at the time, I actually experienced another miracle of the Lord. I was sent to Fort Worth in Shugar, Arizona, to the most difficult training center in the world. The Lord spared me from going overseas, because I had been tested as having a high I.Q. How did I get the high I.Q.? The Lord had blessed me to complete high school in the South, when my parents were alive. Again, the Lord was saving my life, because He had something that He wanted me to do.

Instead of going overseas, I was selected to train the soldiers as they came to Camp Waters for their six-week courses. Every six weeks I had to do everything that the soldiers did. As a result, I was in much better shape than I had ever been. However, it wasn't long before I became tired of all this and could think about nothing but getting out of the army.

I told God that if He would get me out of that place, I would give my life back to Him. The officials set traps and pulled all kinds of tricks to get me on a punishment so that I would have to put in more time, but God miraculously helped me escape all the traps and get out with an honorable discharge.

By the time I reached Chicago, my wife had saved all the money that I had been sending her, and this got us off to a good start. She was wise enough to save it. She hadn't spent it like so many women with husbands in the service had done. My wife was saved and had been going to church while I was in the service.

In those days, I really didn't think about what a coincidence it was that both of our names were George (George and Georgia), and that she had come from the same hometown where I was from, and that she was saved. It didn't occur to me at the time that my wife was also part of God's plan. I got a job working for U.S. Steel and stayed there for 31 years.

At first, I didn't keep my promise to the Lord. I would drive my wife to church, People's Church of God in Christ, where Elder Lawrence Park was pastor. Then I would go and pick her up. However, before long, the Lord began dealing with me.

One Sunday morning, I got dressed. Instead of letting my wife out at the church, as usual, I parked the car and got out. She was surprised. I kept going after that, soon gave my heart to the Lord, and was filled with the Holy Ghost.

I became a pastor in 1973. I have been a pastor for over 20 years.

Remember the days when I was traveling around as a hobo on the trains? Remember the odd jobs that I got here and there? Today, I have been able to use most of the skills I learned in those jobs to help construct the church buildings of Evangelistic Crusaders Church of God in Christ.

We have gone from seven members to 700 members in 20 years. We have a radio ministry and a full schedule of winning souls to Christ every day.

Rev. George Liggins

THE DARK NIGHTS OF LIFE

Dr. James Earl Massey
Job 23:3, 17

"Oh, that I knew where I might find him, that I might come even to his seat!... for I am hemmed in by darkness, and thick darkness covers my face" (Job 23:3, 17, RSV).

There are times in our lives when God seems hidden and strangely absent, even when we call out longingly to Him. Job experienced such a time. Several calamities had befallen Job. He had been deprived of his possessions (Job 1:16). His seven sons and three daughters had been killed when a tornado destroyed the house where they were dining together (1:18-19). Then a hideous disease began to sap his strength (2:7-8). Job's sorrow was deep, and there was no relief from his pain.

Three close friends came to visit but ruined the occasion by accusing Job of having sinned. Those friends could not believe that God would allow a good man to suffer so (Job 4--5).

Anguish. Assaulted on all these fronts, Job cried out, but to no avail. His predicament lingered, and his cry seemed unheard. Job could not understand why God remained silent at such a time in his life. "Oh, that I knew where I might find him," Job exclaimed, "that I might come even to his seat! I would lay my case before him and fill my mouth with arguments. I would learn what he would answer me, and understand what he would say to me. Would he contend with me in the greatness of his power? No; he would give heed to me... and I should be acquitted for ever by my judge" (Job 23:3-7, RSV).

How Job longed to talk with God, but God seemed far away, unavailable for comment, hidden. Job was experiencing a dark night in his life. Hemmed in by that darkness, Job felt unsettled. The dark nights of life always make us feel that way. "Behold, I go forward," Job sighed, "but he is not there; and backward, but I cannot perceive

128

him; on the left hand I seek him, but I cannot behold him; I turn to the right hand, but I cannot see him" (23:8-9).

The Feeling of Unsettlement. Forward, backward, sideways, and still there is no discernible trace of God! The stating of these directions is Job's way of saying how unsettled he felt. A person can become unsettled when unable to locate God. This is particularly true when one is in such need of Him. Job certainly went "forward" in faith by refusing to doubt the justice of the God he knew. However, his unwavering faith had not been honored by a response from God. Therefore he went "backward" in memory, recalling the good times which had now given place to hard times.

Job had many good times to remember. He had an attentive wife, many healthy children, and considerable wealth. He had a good reputation in the community, a circle of admiring friends, good health, and a vital religious life. In the 23rd chapter of Job, we find him looking back on these good times as he talked with three of his friends.

It was in response to a vivid recollection of the good times that Job finally exclaimed, "Oh, that I were as in the months of old, as in the days when God watched over me; when his lamp shone upon my head, and by his light I walked through darkness" (29:2-3).

However, for Job, on that day there was only the bitter contrast. By the 23rd chapter of Job, he was suffering from an ugly set of circumstances, caught in a dark situation, with no light on the horizon, and no word from a strangely silent and seemingly absent God. It was indeed a dark, unsettling night for Job.

Still, Job stepped forward in his faith, believing that the God he knew was just, and he stepped backward in his memory and remained thankful for the good that he already had experienced in life. Job also went "to the left" and asked for help from his friends who, unfortunately, did not present him with a word that seemed reasonable. He went to the "right" by questioning God, but still there was no help and no answer. It was an unsettling experience. Job had done all that he knew to do, but now, at this point, he could do nothing other than wait.

The Question of Undeserved Pain. Job felt that his dark night was undeserved. Indeed, there is nothing in Job's story to suggest that he deserved what was happening to him. Job confessed that he had done nothing in life to offend God or to warrant any vengeance from the Almighty. Job's friends were not so convinced of his innocence. Like many in our time, they believed that living for God meant an exemption from ills. They believed that righteous living would guarantee a steady flow of blessings, such as good health, a steady job, readily answered prayers, and other signs of divine approval.

Job's friends seemed to believe that the godly are exempt from troubles, and that suffering comes only because of what one brings upon oneself. However, Job's friends were wrong in their notions. Undeserved suffering does exist, and the Book of Job highlights its existence in grand fashion. Job's suffering was unsettling and undeserved, but he determined that it would not result in his undoing. He knew that faith is not in vain and true trust is never bankrupt.

Job reasoned that undeserved suffering must have a design and a purpose in it. So after admitting his unsettled state, Job exclaimed: "But [God] knows the way that I take; when he has tried me, I shall come forth as gold" (23:10). The undeserved, dark nights of life are part of a process God uses in the best interests of humankind. Job believed he could endure the process, and if he could not, he would learn the purpose of the suffering beyond his grave.

Therefore he cried, "If a man die, shall he live again? All the days of my service I would wait, till my release should come. Thou wouldest call, and I would answer thee; thou wouldest long for the work of thy hands" (14:14-15).

Even if this was a death wish on Job's part, he uttered it in full faith that goodness must prevail, even if one had to pursue it beyond the grave. Job refused to surrender his hope in God. He determined that trouble would not defeat his spirit.

130

Those who suffer what they believe is undeserved pain must do as Job did. Like Job, they must remember, "[God] knows the way we take" (23:10). The original Hebrew language indicates that Job's expression could read, "He knows how things are with me." Yes, God does know, and one must not forget that when a "dark night" comes. Darkness will not result in one's undoing if one remembers that God is actually present in it and knows how things are. Like Job, one must be certain of the outcome. Job said, "When he has tried me, I shall come forth as gold" (23:10b). With gold, there are degrees of purity and levels of shine. Being processed by God can bring out the best in us and enhance our value, beauty and usefulness.

Feelings of Isolation. The dark nights make us feel isolated. When they come, we are prone to lament, "Nobody knows the trouble I see." There is an aloneness in suffering, a terrifying isolation that the most understanding of friends cannot alter in full. That is why a false assessment by a friend only deepens the tragedy of felt loss and intensifies the misery of one's loneliness.

Job knew that God had no reason to desert him, and that God would operate on his behalf. With this belief, Job uttered a grand statement, signifying audacious faith and an unconquerable spirit:

"For I know that my Redeemer lives, and at last he will stand upon the earth; and after my skin has been thus destroyed, then from my flesh I shall see God, whom I shall see on my side..." (19:25-27a).

Although isolated in circumstances and feeling, Job knew that right must prevail. He therefore refused to despair. His faith gave him the patience to wait.

Waiting for God. President Abraham Lincoln knew what it meant to wait in utter aloneness before God. The period of 1861-62 was a dark time for Lincoln as he prayerfully worked his way through the sharp tensions and internal divisions that plagued the American nation. It was a dark and gloomy time. The nation was in a civil war. Heavy demands were placed on everyone, particularly on Lincoln, the nation's chief executive. Convinced that God was just and that He was not morally indifferent, Lincoln sat at his desk on September, 1862 and prayed about the nation's problems.

He wrote a brief note: "The will of God prevails...I am almost ready to say this is probably true--that God wills this contest, and wills that it shall not end yet. He could have either saved or destroyed the Union without a human contest. Yet the contest began. And it having begun He could give the final victory to either side any day. Yet the contest proceeds."[1]

Lincoln wrote out of an anguished soul. He sensed that a strong Hand was at work within the nation's struggle. While his awareness of this did not expel his anguish, it diminished his anxiety, as he waited on God to complete what was now a lengthy process. It was during Abraham Lincoln's time that the motto "In God we trust" began to appear on the nation's coins. Today that motto is engraved on the walls of the halls where American senators and representatives assemble for business, and it is a tribute to Lincoln's faith, fortitude, and firmness during that long night of trial in the nation's history.

Like nations, individuals also pass through dark times. One of the great promise passages about the Messiah places His coming on a "people who walked in darkness... who dwelt in a land of deep darkness" (Isaiah 9:2). To a nation waiting for Him, the Lord's coming was referred to as "a great light." The Lord knew where His people were. The Lord remembered the people's needs and vindicated their waiting. God always does.

The Crucible. For individuals, families, congregations, groups, or nations, the dark nights of life can be crucibles in which needed cleansing and refinement take place. God wants His people to be like pure gold, and He alone knows the process to use to make that occur. Job viewed God as a great metalworker, refining gold to enhance its beauty, value, and usefulness.

The process God uses is always purposeful. To the person, however, His methods and timing are always problematic. If one looks forward to the end, one will not despair over what occurs in the middle.

Mary McLeod Bethune also knew something about God's mercy in the midst of suffering. She often cautioned African Americans to remember God in times of trials. Calling attention to the Negro spiritual "Nobody Knows the Trouble I See," she explained that those who first sang the song did not stop on a note of complaint. They followed trouble with "Glory Hallelujah."[2] Although they experienced difficulties and had to endure hardships, they looked forward to seeing an end when they would sing "Glory Hallelujah."

People who believe in God will not accept fatalism, despair, or lose hope in the purposes of life. They will continue to bear their burden. They will be sustained by faith that something more must come--something better--because God is God and He is just.

Frederick William Robertson preached often to his parishioners about such a faith. He did so out of his own great suffering while serving the Lord in spiritual loneliness and unrelieved physical pain. In one of his sermons, Robertson urged: "Let life be a life of faith. Do not go timorously about, inquiring what others think, what others believe, and what others say...Believe in God. God is near you. Throw yourself fearlessly upon Him."[3]

That is what Job did. That is what Jesus did when He felt God strangely distant while He was dying on the cross. No night was darker or longer than that awesome hour when He died, with humankind's sins upon His heart. Yes, Jesus was unsettled by His seeming distance from God while He was taking the judgment which should have been taken by humankind!

He was undeserving of that fate. However, He remained unbending in His determination to see it through to the end. Job had also trusted God, looking forward to his vindication. We too can trust, because Jesus, the resurrected Vindicator, is our hope. Job understood that. Therefore, we see his audacious faith and strong will to persevere.

Although God seemed strangely silent, Job believed that he was still in God's care. When the dark nights of life come it is important to remember Job's faith and Jesus' triumph.

BIBLE STUDY APPLICATION

Instructions: Dr. Massey mentioned the "dark night" of Job's trouble. He mentioned that Christians and entire nations have experienced "dark nights." The exercises below provide the opportunity to discover God's power for dealing with the trials of life. There are five exercises, with six questions each. There is a church ministry application question and a personal application question.

1. Dark Nights: In the Beginning

When we meet Job, his life seems in chaos and disorder. In the beginning of time, darkness was associated with chaos and disorder. However, God's Spirit created order out of chaos.

a. What impact did God's power have on the disorder of darkness? (Genesis 1:1)

b. Throughout Scripture, with what has darkness been associated? Explain. (Joel 2:1-2; Micah 3:1-6; Isaiah 8:21--9:1)

c. Throughout Scripture, with what has light (or day)--the opposite of darkness (or night)--been associated? Explain. (Psalm 27:1; John 12; 9:5; Romans 2:19; 12:11)

d. What has God promised, concerning His impact on the darkness of depressing circumstances? (Genesis 1:2-4; Psalm 139; John 8:12; 2 Corinthians 4:6)

e. What are some reasons that God put lights in the sky to deal with darkness? Therefore, what role should religious festivals have in the Christian life? (Genesis 1:14-18)

f. SUMMARY QUESTION: Review your answers to questions a-e. Stretch your imagination. What hope is there for people who are in a personal crisis?

2. Nighttime and the Pillar of Fire

By the 23rd chapter of Job, life had become very difficult for him. In this respect, he had something in common with his ancestors. When life became difficult for the Children of Israel, God made His presence known in a pillar of fire.

a. In Scripture, with what is fire often associated? (Isaiah 4:4; Exodus 3:1-4; 19:16-19; Acts 2:1-4; Hebrews 12:29)

b. How did God make His presence felt in Israel's dark circumstances? (Exodus 13:17-22)

c. What was another way that God showed His presence in darkness? (13:10-16)

d. What was another way that God showed Himself in the midst of dark circumstances? (Acts 1:6-19; 2:1-21)

e. Today, how does the Lord prepare Christians to deal with depressing circumstances? (Matthew 3:11; 1 Corinthians 3:13; Hebrews 1:7; 1 Peter 1:7)

f. SUMMARY QUESTION: Select a period of Black history and consider the role of the African American church in that period. In what ways has the spirit of the African American church been like a pillar of fire?

3. Praising God in the Night (Psalm 22)

Rev. Massey mentions Job's attitude. He had much in common with David. David the psalmist did not wait until his crisis was over to thank and praise God for the outcome.

a. What might have been the nature of David's dark circumstances? (Psalm 22:1-8; 1 Samuel 19:1-2; 21:10-11; 23:14-26)

b. What pleasant memories did David have of God's presence in dark circumstances? (Psalm 22:9-11; 1 Samuel 17:31-37, 41-50)

c. Rev. Massey mentioned ways in which a person can feel hemmed in by circumstances. In what sense was David feeling hemmed in? (1 Samuel 23:14-29; Psalm 22:12-13, 16-17)

    d. What did David have in common with Jesus Christ? (Psalm 22:16-18; Luke 23:26-43; Matthew 27:45-48)

    e. Why did David decide not to wait until the battle was over, but to "shout now"? (Psalm 22:22-31)

    f. SUMMARY QUESTION: In what ways might Christians today follow David's example in dealing with the "dark nights" of their lives?

4. Dealing with the Dangers of the Night (Psalm 91)

Built into the "dark nights" of our circumstances are unseen dangers. However, God helps us deal with the dangers of the night.

    a. What promise has God made concerning hidden dangers of dark circumstances? (Psalm 91:1-3) What are some of these dangers?

    b. What does God's promise mean? (91:4-8)

    c. What promise has God made concerning threats of violence? (91:9-12) What are these threats in modern times?

    d. What promise has God made concerning enemies that strike in the night while one is experiencing a "dark circumstance"? (91:13) Who are some of these enemies in modern times?

    e. What does God promise to believers? (91:14-16; John 3:16, 36; Romans 6:22; Galatians 6:8)

    f. SUMMARY QUESTION: Sometimes adverse circumstances can seem overwhelming. African Americans, in particular, can feel powerless to control some of the dangers facing their communities. Consider your answers to questions a-e. How does Psalm 91 relate to these situations?

5. God, in the Darkness of the Night

Scripture contains images of God's people interacting with Him in the "dark nights" of life.

    a. What causes the righteous person to be able to endure the night? (Psalm 1)

b. What is one way that God speaks to His children in the "dark nights" of life? (Psalm 16)

c. What eases the pain of the "dark nights" of life? (Psalm 42)

d. How does one find comfort during life's trials? (Psalm 77)

e. How does one make contact with God during those periods? (Psalm 88)

f. SUMMARY QUESTION: Does one need to be helpless when one encounters a "dark night" of life? Consider your answers to questions a-e.

6. CHURCH MINISTRY APPLICATION

Sometimes people request counseling when there is no apparent means of resolving a very difficult and painful situation. If someone from your church approached you in such a situation, how would you use the content of this chapter to help the person?

7. PERSONAL APPLICATION

Are you in a seemingly unresolvable difficulty? How can you apply the content of this chapter?

CHAPTER EIGHT

God, in the Struggle

The extended African American family has played an important role in the survival and triumph of Black families. However, when members of extended families advance to middle age, and beyond, illnesses and financial pressures can exhaust the family's resources. Individual family members can become weary and overwhelmed, and the family can collapse under the pressure. Such might have been the case for Vera Shelbon, surrounded by the failing health of her mother, father, children and spouse, and being the only one available to care for them. However, Vera did not collapse; neither did her family. She tells her story below. Following her testimony is a sermon by Dr. J. Alfred Smith, called "An Ash Heap or an Altar?", concerning the grace of God.

In the winter of 1986, my pastor decided to teach the Book of Job at our weekday Bible study. We were into the tenth week of the study when I began to have difficulties of all types.

First of all, my husband, who had cancer, began six weeks of chemotherapy. Each week, he was in the hospital for two days, out for three, and then back for two days. Part of his treatment was that he had to have blood transfusions, which I oversaw at home. During this same period, my mother, who had been sick for quite some time, began to worsen. I had to take care of both of them. It seemed that the ambulance was always coming back and forth to our homes.

At one time, I was driving 67 miles per day, taking my husband back and forth to the Veteran's Administration Hospital, bathing, cooking, cleaning and so forth. I got very little sleep, because some of their care had to be carried out at night.

As a partial solution, I tried to locate a rest home for my mother, but before I could do so, she choked on some meat and had a heart attack. Then, while I was making arrangements to move in with her, the burglar alarm at my house broke and someone robbed my home. What made matters worse is that the insurance company would only pay $8-10,000 of the damages.

I moved in with my mother, only to learn that the extra bathroom I thought we could use did not work. That made caring for her all the more difficult.

Not long after this, my father became ill and needed care. First he had a blood clot that caused him to lose his leg. Then he lost his speech. Then he lost his mind. He could not communicate. He could hardly get from the bed to the commode. After his leg was amputated, he had to be placed in a nursing home. Then he went home to be with the Lord.

Two years later, my 70-year-old mother had another heart attack. This was unexpected. She survived the heart attack but continued to have a series of small strokes. She also lost her mind.

Then my daughter came down with Parkinson's Disease. At the time, she was living with me. She had surgery and began to have tremors in her right hand. At first she thought it might be a nervous condition. However, after she found that it was difficult for her to carry out her daily routine, she went back to the doctor and was diagnosed as having Parkinson's Disease.

I remember being completely exhausted during this time. I also had financial problems which began to escalate. During this period I began to have suicidal thoughts. I even dreamed of ways to kill myself. I was so depressed and exhausted. I can recall that the weather during that period was rainy and dreary. It was all I could do to continue to remind myself that Christians should not commit suicide.

The one bright spot in my life was my weekday Bible class at Allen Temple Baptist Church, only three blocks from my home. The grounds of the church are so beautiful and peaceful. The class met each week on Thursdays, between 7-9:00 p.m., with 100-122 people in attendance. The class was led by my pastor, Dr. J. Alfred Smith. We studied the Book of Job. Just being able to study the book as closely as we did, and reflect on my personal experience, helped me to struggle through my difficulties on a daily basis. My pastor is an excellent teacher. What also helped was that the church became involved in my struggle. The lay ministers visited me, brought communion to my family, and prayed with me.

Without the support of the church, and without my personal fellowship with the Lord, I would not have been able to remain alive. I might very well have yielded to those suicidal dreams that I was having, if it had not been for the Lord on my side.

Today the pressure is still with me, but knowing the Lord in the struggle has made it easier to endure. Both my father and my husband have gone on to be with the Lord. I recently lost one of my granddaughters to AIDS. My mother is in a rest home. However, she recently had another stroke involving her little finger. My daughter with Parkinson's Disease lives with her younger sister. I continue to be involved with the care of both my mother and my daughter.

I wish that there was a special way I could tell my pastor, Dr. J. Alfred Smith, Sr., how much I appreciate his ministry, particularly during that most difficult period of my life. It is hard to express adequately what that weekday Bible study on the Book of Job meant to me and, ultimately, to my family.

Vera Shelbon

AN ASH HEAP OR AN ALTAR?

Dr. J. Alfred Smith
Job 42:1-17

In his first book, Jewish writer Elie Wiesel, who survived the Nazi Holocaust, told of a child whom he witnessed dying on the gallows. The child twisted and turned on the gallows for three days before dying in horror. A voice inside of Wiesel asked, "Where is God?" Another voice answered, "God is on the gallows."

God also sat on the ash heap with Job. What does one do with Job's story that ends like a fairy tale with, "and so they lived happily ever after"? Does one leave Job on the ash heap? Does one argue that Job's restoration simply proves that Eliphaz, Bildad, and Zophar were correct? Does one reason that Job's repentance and return to prosperity prove that sin results in suffering and that righteousness brings blessing? Does Job's restoration to prosperity after repentance prove that Satan was correct when he asked whether Job would worship God if he did not prosper?

Archibald MacLeish explained Job's suffering in another way. He argued that God Himself should take a seat on the ash heap and repent in dust and ashes. MacLeish argued that God needs forgiveness, and human love is the only prospect for love.

Rabbi Harold Duskner, in *When Bad Things Happen to Good People*, drew yet a different conclusion about Job's suffering. He stated that God is limited in power to deal with the suffering of the innocent. He challenged the sufferer to love and asked the victim questions such as:

A) Can you forgive a world which has disappointed you by not being perfect?

B) Can you forgive and love people even if they hurt you by not being perfect?

C) Can you forgive and love God even when God does not measure up to your standards in managing the universe?

Rabbi Duskner challenges the sufferer with additional questions, such as:

A) Have you given up on God?

B) Can you blow on the coals of your hearts and substitute human love for a seeming absence of God's love?

C) Are you trying to escape by merely waiting for the "sweet by and by" of heaven?

D) Are you merely grinning and bearing your painful lot on an ash heap of undeserved suffering?

Humility and Graciousness. Let's examine Job more closely. Notice that Job did not respond in any of the four ways just mentioned. In Job 42:5-6 he says: "In the past I knew only what others had told me, but now I have seen you with my own eyes. So I am ashamed of all I have said and I repent in dust and ashes" (TEV). Job repented! Job made no claim to personal righteousness. He humbled himself to receive the gift of God's grace.

Job's next move was to offer grace to his three friends who had unjustly attacked him. Job 42:10 says, "After Job prayed for his friends, the Lord made him prosperous again" (NIV). Job almost gave up on God, but God never gave up on Job. God's grace to Job was a free gift that Job had to learn to accept. This was not easy. As a rich member of the upper class, Job accepted God's grace by paying the expensive response of repentance. He then gave grace to his friends who falsely attacked him. Job's encounter with the God of grace left Job seeking no revenge. It required grace to pray for persons by whom he had been betrayed.

Grace holds no grudges. Job 42:11 says, "All his brothers and sisters and everyone who had known him before came to him and ate with him in his house. They comforted and consoled him over all the trouble the Lord had brought upon him, and each one gave him a piece of silver and a gold ring" (NIV).

How sad, how sickening! How typical of life! When one's fortune falls, often one is deserted by family and friends. However, when one's fame rises, family and "fair weather" friends come to comfort and console. People come when one doesn't need them, but grace prevents one from asking, "Where were you when I needed you?"

God's Grace. God brought prosperity into Job's life with more grace. God took Job off the ash heap! That was grace! Let's take a closer look at what God did for Job.

God doubled Job's blessings, but Job's number of daughters remained the same. The names of Job's daughters are very significant. Jemimah means turtledove or "beautiful in song". Keziah means cinnamon, the most fragrant of the spices, or "beautiful in smell". Keren-Happauch means "horn of paint," or cosmetics, or "beautiful in sight". In other words, God caused Job to see beauty in things he may have taken for granted before.

Job's reaction to his daughters symbolizes how God reacts to us in our needs. To each of his three daughters, Job gave an inheritance equal to that of their brothers. In a patriarchal age in which women did not count for as much as men, Job demonstrated grace within his gender and family relationships. God also gave Job 14 sons. In this gift, God fulfilled a promise He had made to Abraham--that his seed would be multiplied as the stars of the sky and as the sand of the sea (Genesis 11:1-3).

In a patriarchal age, grace gives to women. In an adult-run culture, grace gives to children. In an affluent society, grace gives to the poor. In a macho world, grace gives to the weak. In a Jewish nation, grace gives to Gentiles. In a Christian community, grace gives to sinners. Job's daughters symbolized the Gentiles, who did not share the promise given to Abraham and were outside of Job's spiritual inheritance. Job broke the tradition and taught us that grace has no favorites. The story of Job is an illustration of the grace of God.

BIBLE STUDY APPLICATION

Instructions: Dr. Smith mentioned that Job's life is an illustration of the grace of God. The exercises below provide the opportunity to study the grace of God more closely. There are five exercises, with six questions each. Then there is a church ministry application question and a personal application question.

1. Compassion, Patience and Love: Aspects of God's Grace

Graciousness involves compassion, patience, love and commitment.
a. List three features of God's grace. (Exodus 34:1-7)
b. Under what circumstances did Moses remember characteristics of God's grace? (Numbers 14:1-22)
c. In what circumstance did the psalmist remember God's grace? (Psalm 86, especially verses 15-16)
d. What is a circumstance in which a prophet remembered God's grace? (Joel 2:1-14)
e. Why was Jonah uncomfortable with God's grace? (Jonah 4:1-11)
f. SUMMARY QUESTION: Can you think of specific 20th century examples of God's compassion, patience and unconditional love? In Job's life, how did God show patience, love and compassion?

2. Expressions of God's Grace

Grace is more than an attitude. It is an action. God demonstrated His grace by taking actions to protect the poor, oppressed and mentally ill.
a. What was one expression of God's grace? (Exodus 19:24--20:2; 22:21-27)
b. What was another expression of God's grace? (Psalm 30:1-12)
c. What was another expression of God's grace? (Psalm 103:1-10)

145

d. What was another expression of God's grace? (Isaiah 30:19-26)

e. What was yet another expression of God's grace? (Exodus 14:1-32)

f. SUMMARY QUESTION: Can you think of an expression of God's grace in African American history? Explain.

3. God's Grace and Salvation

God demonstrated His compassion, love and patience when He sent His Son Jesus to die for the sins of humankind.

a. What is one way that Jesus is an expression of God's grace? (2 Corinthians 5:20--6:2)

b. What is another way that Jesus is an expression of God's grace? (Romans 5:12-19)

c. What is another way that Jesus is an expression of God's grace? (Ephesians 3:14-20)

d. What is a way that the life of the Apostle Paul is an expression of God's grace? (1 Timothy 1:12-17)

e. What is yet another expression of God's grace? (Acts 15:1-11)

f. SUMMARY QUESTION: Consider your answers to questions a-e. How is your life an expression of God's grace?

4. Grace for Ministry

God demonstrates His compassion and kindness by giving us the privilege and power to carry out His ministry on earth.

a. What is one of God's gracious gifts to the believer? (Romans 12:1-5)

b. What is another of God's gracious gifts to the believer? (Romans 12:6-8)

c. What is one way that, taken collectively, Christian ministers are expressions of God's grace? To whom? (1 Corinthians 3:5-13)

d. How do Christians become expressions of God's grace? (1 Peter 4:7-11)

146

e. How is the Church an expression of God's grace? (Matthew 5:13-16)

f. SUMMARY QUESTION: What is your ministry in your church and your family? Compare and contrast your ministry with the ministry that Job had. How is your ministry an expression of God's grace?

5. Responding to God's Grace

One cannot fully appreciate God's grace if one does not respond appropriately to it.

a. What is one way of responding to God's grace? (Romans 14:6)

b. What is another way to respond to God's grace? (1 Corinthians 10:31-33)

c. What is another way to respond to God's grace? (Philippians 4:4-6)

d. What is another way to respond to God's grace? (Hebrews 13:15-16)

e. What is yet another way to respond to God's grace? (Philippians 1:9-11)

f. SUMMARY QUESTION: Consider the testimony of Vera Shelbon. In what ways is it an expression of God's grace?

6. CHURCH MINISTRY APPLICATION

Consider the history of your local church and that of your family. Can you name specific expressions of God's grace in those histories? How might older members of your church share stories about the church's history--stories that are expressions of God's grace?

7. PERSONAL APPLICATION

In what specific ways do you respond to God's grace in your life?

CHAPTER NINE

A Woman With an Issue of Blood

The birth of every infant is a miracle, particularly when one considers the complexity of the nine-month birthing process itself--a process that is fraught with life-threatening dangers to the mother and child. It is even more obvious when the mother encounters a life-threatening complication, and overcomes it with the power of God. Such was the experience of Rev. Diana Bradey Timberlake. While giving birth to her son, she became a modern woman "with an issue of blood," a participant and eye-witness to the healing power of God. Through it all, she learned that Jesus is the answer.

Following is her testimony and a sermon by her, based on Psalm 30. In it, she talks about the physical, spiritual and emotional healing power of God.

When I was 21 years old, I went into the hospital in preterm labor. My bag of waters had broken and I was only eight months pregnant, and you know how the old folks say, "Eight month babies often times don't make it." Well, after an 11 hour and 38 minute labor, I had a baby boy who weighed 5 lbs. 3 oz. My husband was told everything was fine and that he could leave. So he left to celebrate and I went to the recovery room.

Within minutes, I began to hemorrhage. They took me back to the delivery room to examine me and find the source of the bleeding. But, they couldn't determine the cause. They started drawing blood for tests, at 3:00 a.m. on Wednesday, March 15, 1979. As the time ticked away, I started to pray.

Why that hadn't occurred to me before, I don't know. Perhaps it was because time was running out. Maybe it was because I put my faith in me when I stopped going to church, or maybe it was because I put my faith in the doctors, but whatever the reason, time was running out. I had nowhere else to turn and so I prayed. What is important is that I prayed that the Lord would save me this one time and let me see my son grow up. I promised that I would love the Lord and serve Him for the rest of my life.

I heard a voice in the distance. I asked the people in the room with me to hush, because somebody was calling my name. I listened to the voice approaching from afar, but the voice was unfamiliar and I couldn't tell who it was. I called out, "Who's calling me?" But the doctors and nurses thought I was going into shock and was beginning to hallucinate. One of the nurses called out that my blood pressure had dropped to 50/0. They were working vigorously around me, and the warm blood was now gushing from my body. My mother, who was standing next to the bed, held my hand tightly and said, "Baby, don't answer, don't answer the voice that's calling you." You see, the old folks believed that when you have a baby, death passes your bed nine times, and if you reach out to death any one of those times, then you'll die.

Jesus came with a voice soft like a summer breeze rumbling through the trees, calling my name. He came as a light brighter than the sun, that lit up that room like a new paint job, with a heat that radiated so warm that perspiration ran down my face. In the door stood the Lord in all of His glory and splendor. He said,

EVERYTHING WILL BE ALL RIGHT. Suddenly He was gone, but not really, and the hemorrhaging stopped, as suddenly as it had started.

The doctors called it a medical miracle. The nurses said I was lucky, but I said that surely the Lord, the very Son of God was in this place and He saved me. He saved me, in the ordinary. He saved me in the reality of a hospital room where the doctors said it was all over. He saved me. Yes, Jesus is the answer!

Rev. Diana Timberlake

THE ANSWER IS JESUS

Rev. Diana Timberlake
Psalm 30

Have you ever been in a situation where you didn't know what to do and there was no visible or logical way out? When no one could fix it or even patch it up for a while? Where you were so consumed with your misery or a problem, that you become too blind to see options, too deaf to hear what the Spirit of the Lord had to say, too numb to feel the gentle tug of the Holy Spirit trying to lead you the way God would have you go? Well, that's where the author of Psalm 30 had been and was delivered from in this psalm of thanksgiving. This is the story of a believer's life-saving, mind-changing experience with God, and his fragmented, prophetic glimpse of the saving grace of Jesus.

The setting is in the temple, probably during the part of the service we commonly call devotions, because he's testifying about the saving grace of God. Just like when we witness the power of God in our lives, get "filled up" and start praising the Lord for what He has done for us.

151

In the first three verses, the psalmist says he will exalt, lift up, the Lord, because his God raised him from a deadly sickness and from the callous rejoicing of his enemies over his misfortune. For Sheol and the Pit are synonyms for death (30:1-3).

In the next two verses (30:4-5), the psalmist invites worshipers gathered in the temple to join his songs of praise for God. God's wrath is a secondary and transient aspect of His nature, and His true and permanent purpose for humankind is grace and favor. But, before the actual singing of the songs of praise started, the psalmist witnesses some more (30:6-10), this time from the vantage point of having been delivered as the psalmist looks back on his trouble.

In good times he had been proud and self-satisfied. Perhaps to teach him humility, God withdrew His protecting presence and he fell desperately ill. In any event, he appealed to God on the grounds that since the dead cannot praise God, his passing into the Pit would be all loss and no gain for the Lord (30:6-10).

In the next two verses (30:11-12), he acknowledges that his prayer was abundantly answered. God completely reversed his condition of misery, giving him a festive robe instead of the sackcloth garment of the mourner. He is sure that his new state will be permanent, on his soul forever.

This passage of Scripture was astonishing for me. As I prayerfully read through it, an eerie feeling of "de ja vu" came over me. The reason was because this was my story, written by someone I don't even know, thousands of years before I was born. The thing that struck me the strangest was the psalmist alludes that the answer for his troubles was God, and the answer for my problem was Jesus. Now that may not seem like a great difference to you, but for a story that was actually my story, the answer had to be Jesus.

The psalmist, who wrote this hundreds of years before the birth of Jesus, couldn't possibly have known about Jesus, I thought, and then the Spirit of the Lord showed me something I had missed over and over again, probably like many of you.

The Holy Spirit showed me eight points in this passage of Scripture: In the first verse, the psalmist was lifted up just like Jesus does us. Jesus had a specific anointing and mission on earth, which He so clearly explains in Luke 4:18-19. He was sent to preach the Gospel to the poor and deliverance to the captives. He was sent to heal the brokenhearted and give sight to the blind. He was sent to liberate the oppressed. And that's lifting in and of itself.

Acute, chronic, terminal illness leaves us brokenhearted and poor in spirit. We become captives of medicines and treatments after we're home bound and more times than not, mentally burdened. We become blind to the blessings in the life we have left. We often become depressed and beat down by rising medical costs and physical and mental limitations of the illness. It is to us that Jesus comes.

Jesus lifts us up by healing our brokenheartedness, by delivering us from the chains and restrictions in our minds due to physical limitations. He lifts us up by giving us insight into the value of life and the significance of having one more day, to glorify the Father, to enjoy our loved ones, to set our business in order, and to repent. Then He lifts us up by taking our burdens of oppression and leaving us in a state of freedom.

As I laid on my hospital bed, literally hours from death, I found myself hoping and praying for one more chance. One more chance to tell my loved ones how much I loved and appreciated them, one more chance to see my only child, my newborn baby grow into a decent and good human being, just one more chance to do something worthwhile in my own life. And although I didn't know it at the time, I did just what James 4:10 suggested. I humbled myself in the sight of the Lord and He did lift me up.

In Psalm 30:2, the healing power mentioned was for me, the same as when Jesus healed Peter's mother-in-law in Mark 1, the paralytic in Mark 2, the man with the withered hand in Mark 3, and the woman with the issue of blood in Mark 5.

These are but a few displays of the healing power of Jesus, but what makes these significant is that: 1) They all remained nameless, but not forgotten. 2) They are examples of various stages of the disease process. (Peter's mother-in-law had an acute or sudden illness of fever. The paralytic had an irreversibly permanent condition, the man with the withered hand had a degenerative or chronic condition, and the woman with the issue of blood had a long-term disease.) Yet all were healed. 3) These were regular, ordinary people like you and me, with common illnesses and diseases that Jesus healed, primarily because they believed, or had faith enough in Him to be able to set them free, to liberate them from their bondage of illness. Doctors couldn't cure them, but Jesus could.

In Psalm 30:3, we see the power of Jesus to not only heal the sick, but we also see His extraordinary power to restore life by the raising of the destined dead. Just like Jesus did to Jarius's daughter in Mark 5, Lazarus in John 11, and the widow of Nain's son in Luke 7. It is in our illness that we contemplate and fear death the most. Death is oftentimes what we fear as the last and final stage of our illness and of life. Death is the permanent condition of our physical bodies, and no one or nothing else can help.

But with Jesus, death can be a short nap, a long sleep, or eternal bliss. This is evident in the power and passion of Jesus when He raises these people from the dead. Jarius's 12-year-old daughter had been dead but a short time, the widow's son was in the coffin during the funeral procession, and Lazarus had been buried four days. But as diverse as the amount of time each had been dead, for Jesus, it was a matter of speaking the Word, and they were restored to life. In other words, Jesus our Saviour can and does save us, restore us and redeem us. He is the God of another chance.

The fourth verse of Psalm 30 reveals the importance that God places on Jesus, by our remembrance of His holy name, for there is no other name under the heavens given among men by which

154

we must be saved (Acts 4:12). There is no one in the history of the world that can save us, any of us, except Jesus the Christ-- not doctors or nurses, not lawyers or judges, not government officials or scientists. They can treat us and defend us, they can even inform us, but they can't heal us or save us. I had put my faith in man, and when man failed me, I turned to God, and Jesus the Son of the living God heard and answered my cry.

As the Holy Spirit worked in me, I could feel the excitement rising, and in Psalm 30:5 the joy of God is revealed to us, just as the joy of the morning is the light. John 1 tells us that Jesus is the Light of the world. Jesus is our Light, leading us out of the darkness of pain, fear, hopelessness, and helplessness. We can feel that joy in the midst of turmoil. By His stripes, we are healed.

When the doctors said I wouldn't make it until morning the darkness that overshadowed me was devastating. I can imagine it is much like the darkness that overshadows many of you when doctors tell you that your illness is terminal, or that the cancer is spread too much for surgery to help or there's nothing else they can do. But I'm here to tell you, Jesus can bring light in the midst of that darkness. He can heal you. He can cure you and make you whole.

I know He can do it for you because He did it for me. Me, a sinner, but saved by the blood of Jesus. The morning light was a joy for me to behold, when I thought I would never again see the sunlight or feel its warm rays. In fact, every day with Jesus is sweeter than the day before. So I say to you, if you've already sought doctors, medicines and treatments, don't lose hope. Don't give up and don't give out. Try Jesus. Matthew 7:7 says, "Ask, and it shall be given you; seek, and ye shall find; knock, and it shall be opened unto you."

The sixth point is found in Psalm 30:7. As the Holy Spirit convicts your way, Jesus empowers you to be steadfast like a mountain, where you will not be moved. Jesus empowers us with the Holy Spirit. He provides strength to endure our misfortunes and temptations, He provides guidance in the way and will of God, and He provides comfort in the knowledge that we are not alone, because He is with us.

Verse nine brings us to the seventh point, the declaration of the truth. God revealed His truth in the death, resurrection, and ascension of His only begotten Son, Jesus Christ. God will also reveal the truth in your deliverance. What is the truth, you ask? The truth is God's undying, eternal love for you and me, made manifest in His Son, Jesus Christ. It was because of God's love that He sent His Son from the heavens, in the flesh, that we could be saved and have life.

Last, but certainly not least, the eighth point is found in verse 11. You too can be the prodigal son. Luke 15 is an illustration of how you can always come home again and the Father will be waiting to bring you in. God wants us to love, trust, believe and depend on Him. God can and has provided for all of our needs. We have but to ask. God wants that none of us should perish.

That spells Jesus--the Way, the Truth and the Life. There is power in the name of Jesus, power to lift you and love you, power to heal you and save you, power to deliver you and liberate you, power to comfort and console, THERE IS POWER. Jesus said He will be with us always, even to the end of the earth. Jesus is the Light of the world. Who gives you life and gives it more abundantly? Jesus. Jesus will heal you and love you.

Jesus is the answer. Jesus is the answer because He went to Calvary and died that we might live. Jesus is the answer when He defeated Satan in the depths of hell and took the keys. Jesus is the answer in the Resurrection when, on the third day, the Father raised Him up. Jesus is the answer when He ascended to the right hand of the Father. Nor is there salvation in any other. God so loved the world that He gave His only begotten Son, that whosoever believeth on Him would not perish, but have everlasting life (John 3:16).

For God did not send His Son into the world to condemn the world, but that the world through Him might be saved. Nobody took His life, He laid it down freely for you and me. When the Son set you free, you're free indeed. Yes, Jesus is the answer.

I'm so glad to be here telling you about the saving grace and power of Jesus. I know it because He saved me. I'm so glad to tell you that the psalmist knew it, but what I want to know is, do you know it? Do you know that Jesus is the answer? Try Him for yourself.

"God has highly exalted Him and given Him the name which is above every name, that at the name of Jesus every knee should bow, of those in heaven, and those on earth, and of those under the earth, and every tongue should confess that Jesus Christ is Lord, to the glory of God the Father" (Philippians 2:9-11). Hold fast to the word of life.

This passage of Scripture points to all of us. In a spiritual sense, we all were lost and dead in sin. Our very society holds us tightly in the ropes of bondage, and each at different times and different levels, which, as it turns out is our darkness. The bondage of racism, the bondage of sexism, and the bondage of classism have left chains of slavery on our minds.

But the good news is that there is joy in the morning, and through Jesus Christ we are freed. Freed up to love ourselves as God has made us, men and women, black and white, brown and yellow. Freed up from the bonds of society that tell us materialism determines classism. We are free and we are rich in the blood of Jesus Christ the Liberator. Jesus liberates sickness with healing, Jesus liberates death with life. Jesus liberates us from racism and sexism when we were made in the image of the Father. Jesus liberates classism with the overflowing gifts of the Spirit. The God Triune is Mother for the motherless and Father for the fatherless. The triune God is Spouse for the spouseless and Friend for the friendless. We are not alone, for Jesus is with us always, even until the end of the time.

My weeping had literally endured for a night, and I had a great joy in the morning. Yes, for me the answer is Jesus. The Lord answered my prayer abundantly and He answered it personally. That was 14 years 1 month 27 days and 18 hours ago (from this writing), and I'm here to tell you, Jesus is the answer.

He did for me and He'll do it for you. Won't you let Jesus in your life.

No matter what the problem; whether it's illness or finances, spouse or children, whether it's at home or work, school or play, whether it's in the city or in the country, in the "big house" or in the White House, or even in no house at all. Let it go and let God. God gave us the answer. Jesus is the answer, Jesus can fix it, Jesus sweet Jesus, is the answer.

What a friend we have in Jesus,
All our sins and griefs to bear!
What a privilege to carry,
Everything to God in prayer!
O what peace we often forfeit,
O what needless pain we bear,
All because we do not carry,
Everything to God in prayer![1]

BIBLE STUDY APPLICATION

Instructions: Rev. Timberlake mentioned that the author of Psalm 30 experienced a type of healing that was similar to the healings that many other people have experienced from the Lord. The exercises below provide the opportunity to study the Lord's healing power. There are five exercises, with six questions each. Then there is a church ministry application question and a personal application question.

1. Kidney Disease, Malaria and Typhoid Fever (Matthew 8:14-15; Mark 1:29-31)

No doubt, Peter's mother-in-law was in a situation where there was no visible or logical way out. When Jesus found her, perhaps she had become a victim of malaria, typhoid fever, or one of the kidney diseases that were epidemic in Capernaum at the time.

a. What did Peter's mother-in-law have in common with a Roman centurion's son? (John 4:43-54) How did Jesus help?

b. What did Peter's mother-in-law have in common with Pubius's father? (Acts 28:7-8) How did Jesus help?

c. What role did relatives and friends play in the healing of people with high fevers? (Mark 1:29-31; John 4:43-54; Acts 28:7-8)

d. What are some 20th century diseases that are similar to the ones mentioned in the Scriptures of questions a-c? Which ones are still without cures today?

e. In what sense did God have a reputation as a healer of the Israelites? Explain. (Deuteronomy 32:39) In what sense does He have a reputation for being a healer among African Americans? Explain.

f. SUMMARY QUESTION: What are the similarities and differences between the stories of the healings of the people mentioned in questions a-e? Is God still healing people today? Explain.

2. Strokes, Epilepsy, Polio and Paralysis

Both today and yesterday people with diseases such as those mentioned here were often consumed by their misery.

a. What are some instances of paralysis that have been brought on by strokes in the Old Testament? (1 Samuel 25:36-38; Psalm 137:5-6; 2 Kings 4:18-20)

b. What are some New Testament instances of paralysis that could have been brought on by strokes? (Matthew 4:23-25; Luke 6:6-10; Mark 3:1-5)

c. What is a possible instance of epilepsy in the Bible? (Luke 9:37-43)

d. What may have impressed Jesus about the friends of the paralyzed man? (Matthew 9:1-2; Mark 2:1-4)

e. How did the paralyzed man demonstrate his faith? (Luke 5:25-26)

f. SUMMARY QUESTION: Using Psalm 30 and the story of the paralyzed man as background, explain why there is hope for paralyzed people today.

3. Female Sicknesses

In the Mosaic Law, women who had discharges or gynecological problems of any kind were considered unclean.

a. What were some of the ancient restrictions placed on women who had lengthy menstrual flows? (Leviticus 15:25-30)

b. How were women with normal menstrual periods treated? (Leviticus 15:19-24; Ezekiel 36:16-17)

c. How were women treated immediately after childbirth? (Leviticus 12:1-8)

d. Considering your answers to questions a-c, why might the woman in Mark 5 have "trembled with fear" when she touched Jesus and was discovered? (Mark 5:25-34)

e. Explain why the rules mentioned in questions a-c are no longer in effect among Christians. (Hebrews 8:7-12; 10:1-10)

f. SUMMARY QUESTION: Compare and contrast the stories of the woman with the issue of blood in Mark 5 with that of Rev. Timberlake. Is Jesus still healing people today? Explain.

4. God, the Extender of Life

In a number of places throughout Scripture, people on their death bed cried out to God and God extended their lives.

a. Under what circumstances did God extend Hezekiah's life? (2 Kings 20:1-11)

b. Under what circumstances did God extend the psalmist's life? (Psalm 41:1-13)

c. Under what circumstances did God heal Jeremiah emotionally and thereby extend his life? (Jeremiah 15:10-21)

d. Name some of the ways in which the Lord healed people by extending their lives in various circumstances. (Psalm 107:1-43)

e. In what sense did the psalmist decide not to wait until the battle was over, but to "shout now?" (Psalm 30)

f. SUMMARY QUESTION: Can you recall times when people have been close to death and God has miraculously extended their lives? In what ways are their stories similar to that of Rev. Timberlake?

5. Prayer for the Sick

Throughout the stories of Jesus healing the sick, relatives and friends played an important part in their healings.

a. What role did friends and relatives play in the story of a mute man? (Matthew 9:32-33)

b. What role did friends and relatives play in the healing of a blind man? (Matthew 12:22-23)

c. What role did a mother play in the healing of her daughter? (Matthew 15:21-28)

d. What role did a father play in the healing of his son? (Matthew 17:14-20)

e. What role did the sisters of Lazarus play in Lazarus's resurrection from the dead? (John 11:1-44)

f. SUMMARY QUESTION: There are many debilitating illnesses in the African American community today. What roles can the church play in bringing about healing?

6. CHURCH MINISTRY APPLICATION

What people in what ministries or auxiliaries in your church are in contact with people who are physically ill? How can the content of this chapter help them in carrying out their ministries?

7. PERSONAL APPLICATION

Are you or a loved one physically ill? How can you use the content of this chapter for hope and healing?

CHAPTER TEN

A Saved Life

Among the results of sin are guilt, confusion, powerlessness and a feeling of alienation from God. These feelings often distract us from the image of our merciful God who forgives, heals and is willing to engage in a covenant relationship with us. However, our salvation does not depend entirely on our ability to see God in a moment of confusion. God reaches out to us, through the circumstances of our lives, and gradually draws us, while still delegating the decision to respond, to us.

That is the healing mercy of God. Robert Rooker experienced that mercy. He was submerged in guilt, powerlessness and confusion, but God reached out to him, in the context of his world, and Robert made the decision to respond. His testimony is printed below. Following it is a sermon by Dr. Frank Madison Reid on God's healing mercy.

I was born in the middle of a crisis, but I didn't know it. I might have become just another victim of circumstances, if I had not reached out to the Lord.

The crisis involved my uncle, the dangerous life he lived, and the fact that I wanted to be just like him. From as far back as I can remember, perhaps even when I was four or five years old, I had admired my uncle. He was the only man I knew who could change clothes five times in the same day. He was the best-dressed and best-looking man I knew. He also had plenty of girlfriends, who were also well-dressed and good-looking. However, as I was growing up, I did not fully understand the significance of the fact that my uncle got his money from the sale of illegal drugs, that he used drugs, and that he employed prostitutes. I guess I didn't fully understand what all of that really meant.

By the time I was 12 years old, I was in the business too. I used to steal drugs from my uncle, sell them, and use the money to get more drugs to sell. Then I would purchase clothes. It wasn't long before I had my own prostitutes working for me. I hid this from my uncle, because he had told me that he did not want me to get into that type of business.

I will never forget the night one of my uncle's lady friends told me that he had died. My uncle had been sick for about six months, but somehow I was in a state of denial. To me, my uncle was invincible. I did not expect him to die of a hemorrhage directly related to the drugs he had been using. I left the county hospital in a state of shock. I was only 19 years old at the time.

Then I really plunged myself into the drug culture of the streets. I wanted to be able to turn over money the same way my uncle did. I also began to use drugs heavily. I watched myself steadily decline physically and mentally. Before long, I had done time in prison and I was physically ill. I remember that all I wanted was to somehow get free of drugs, but I didn't know how.

Then, somehow, people began to appear almost out of nowhere-- people who had been a part of the street drug scene. However, they looked so much better. They seemed healthier. When I asked them what had happened to them, they told me that they had been in a drug rehabilitation center in Tinley Park, Illinois.

I went to the center and enrolled. It was a therapeutic community. My decision to get treatment was the best decision I had made in a long time. It was then that gradually, I began to turn to

God. One of my strongest memories of this time is one night, when I had a vision of my body as a piece of Swiss cheese. In the vision, I picked out pieces of my body which I did not consider to be of any value. After a while, I had taken so many pieces out that the only image left was that of a ball of Swiss cheese that would not bounce.

As I remained in the program, I began to see myself change and become more whole. I did not yet belong to a church. However, gradually I lost my fascination with flashy clothing. I began to relax for the first time in my life. I lost interest in the street life, and I lost interest in prostitutes and prostitution. I did not have any more use for the street life.

Somewhere during this time, small groups of people from the center began to go to church on Sundays. I remember thinking that I would go with them just to get away from the grounds. However, gradually I became fascinated with what took place within the sanctuary. The people said that they were sanctified and filled with the Holy Ghost. The sanctified women seemed so holy. The music was so powerful. The more that I attended church, the more I was drawn to the people and to the Lord. I soon gave my life to the Lord. Then I ended up marrying a Pentecostal woman, my beautiful wife, Michelle.

Not long after that, I got a job that didn't involve selling drugs. As a part of the Tinley Park program, I was hired in a position in Rockford, Illinois. Nine people applied for the job, and they narrowed the qualified applicants down to two. Then the field narrowed to me. My new job at the ARC (Addiction Rehabilitation Center) gave me a new chance in life.

I worked very hard, turning the job I had into a directorship, and founding a live-in program and a day care program for people struggling to overcome addictions. Since that time I have written an autobiography which is being considered for publication by a publishing company in Chicago.

Today, I am struggling with kidney failure, and have other physical illnesses which may be complications from the days when I used drugs. I have been in and out of the hospital many times, and I have no guarantee of what my immediate future will be. Just this week, I lost a son to pneumonia. Even though my life is not problem-free, today is much different from yesterday because today I know the Lord. The Lord saved my life. I do not know where I would be if it had not been for Him. As far as I am concerned, knowing Jesus is enough for me. I don't need anything more than that.

Robert Rooker

GOD'S HEALING MERCY

Dr. Frank Madison Reid
Psalm 51

This chapter is about the healing power of the mercy of God. King David the psalmist was one of the giants of the Old Testament. He was the youngest of his father's children. He was the child who exceeded all of his parents' expectations. While still a child he received the anointing of God. One does not have to be an adult to receive the Spirit of God. Because God had put His hands on David from an early age, David did great things. The king sent for young David, the musical prodigy, because he had heard about the soothing music that David could play. It was music that could calm the savage soul and the savage beast that lurked within King Saul.

Young David was both a child prodigy and a warrior for God. When the adults were afraid to stand against the giant Goliath, David testified that the same God who had delivered David's sheep from the lions and bears would deliver Goliath into David's hands. David asked the Israelite soldiers who this Philistine giant was, to believe that he could stand before the living

166

God.

David was a child prodigy and a young man of God-like courage and conviction. When God uses a person while s/he is young, God has a plan for the person when s/he becomes older. Everything that happened to David when he was young prepared him to lead God's people.

When selecting the first king of Israel, people had based their choice on popularity and good looks. However, David, the second leader of Israel, was chosen and anointed by God. When Saul met his dastardly end, God selected David to be the next leader of Israel. He selected David whom He had prepared for the position of leading the people of God.

However, when God makes a person successful, the person needs to pray. The person needs to pray increasingly because success is dangerous. The more successful God makes the person, the more blessings God gives the person, the angrier the devil, the adversary becomes. That is why the world says power corrupts. In some ways, even spiritual power can corrupt. If one is not careful, one can become so caught up in high spiritual heights that one can be tempted to take one's eyes off God and take personal credit for the things of God.

Recall that King David, from the time he was a child, had been a great man of courage, had won many battles, and had written many wonderful songs to God, but he had to learn firsthand that power can corrupt. One day when David's troops were out fighting and he should have been at war, David was at home in Jerusalem, up on his roof, watching a beautiful woman by the name of Bathsheba. Bathsheba was alone bathing, minding her own business when David saw her, took her, and had sex with her. David, the man after God's own heart, saw Bathsheba and made love to her. This was David, the man anointed by God, the man who knew how God had blessed him from childhood, who broke God's law.

After he broke God's law by sleeping with Bathsheba (the wife of one of his most loyal servants), he lied about it. Sin is a

167

problem. Either a person faces it up front or the person has to cover it up. The more one covers sin, the worse it becomes.

For David, it was bad enough to sleep with Bathsheba, but then he made it worse by lying about it, and then by killing Uriah, Bathsheba's husband. David's sin just kept on growing, from one sin to another. David committed adultery. Then he lied. Then he committed murder.

David thought he had escaped any penalty for sin. In this sense, David was like many Christians sinning today. When one sins, one often believes that s/he can get away with it. However, all one has to do is continue living. Judgment day will come. Whatever one does in the dark, comes to the light. One may escape the penalty for a while, but eventually the penalty will come.

That is what happened to David. One day Nathan the prophet told David a story about a ruler who had many sheep and great riches. This ruler saw one poor member of his kingdom who had only one baby lamb. The king took the lamb and used it as food for one of his feasts. When David asked Nathan who had done such a thing, Nathan told David that he was the person who had committed the sin. The brokenhearted David wrote the 51st psalm.

There are parallels in David's story between his plight and the plight of African Americans. Recall that America was a stepchild, born out of powerful England. It was a nation not only of pilgrims, but of pimps and prostitutes, who were not wanted in England. Originally America was a nation of prisoners. Do not be mistaken that every white person who came over on the Mayflower was from a lineage of princes and kings. Study the history. Many of these people were pimps, prostitutes, prisoners and murderers who came here because they were not wanted anywhere in England.

In spite of the fact that God put His hands on the land to which they came, these pimps and prostitutes remained evil. During the 1700s they fought against England for their freedom, but they continued to oppress Black people. All during this time they were creating harsh slave laws. They kept Black people in bondage and stole the land of Native Americans.

In spite of that, God blessed America. However, the more God blessed America, the more oppressive America became. Then when America became a mature world power, along came World War II. Hitler became a threat to America. However, America did not drop a nuclear bomb on Hitler. Instead, America bombed a people who did not look like them. It was racism that caused them to bomb Japan. But look what God has done! The Japan that was bombed some 50 years ago, now has America economically laying at its feet. There is healing power in the mercies of God!

David recognized that healing power. Recalling God's mercy and recalling his sin, David cried unto the Lord, "Have mercy upon me, O God, according to thy loving kindness: according unto the multitude of thy tender mercies blot out my transgressions" (51:1, KJV). David understood that regardless of how powerful he was, he needed to ask God for mercy.

What does God's mercy have to do with Rodney King? Rodney King is a symbol of 400 years of racism, sexism, and economic inequality. George Bush needed to do more than send troops to Los Angeles. George Bush needed to declare a national day of mourning. Americans needed to ask God to have mercy, not only for what they had done to Rodney King, but for what they had done to the young Black girl who was shot by a Korean. Americans need to ask mercy for 10 million Africans whose bones are at the bottom of the Atlantic Ocean. America needs to ask God to have mercy for the Black women who were raped, and the Black men who were castrated throughout the history of America. America needs to ask God to have mercy on them for taking money out of the mouths of children, and for taking money from Head Start programs and giving it to major corporations. America needs to ask God to have mercy.

The problem is much bigger than Rodney King. How many Rodney Kings have there been over the last 400 years? How many Black men have been lynched? How many sit in jail unjustly? African American and Hispanic young men are being called looters. However, who are the real thugs? Are the real thugs those who broke into shops in Los Angeles and Atlanta, or are the real thugs those who wear business suits and stole billions of dollars from the savings and loans of this nation? Who are the real thugs? If the children who loot are thugs, they are following examples of rich and privileged thugs of this nation.

There is also a whole class of African Americans that needs to ask God to have mercy. It is that group of African Americans whom God has blessed with education and material benefits. God did not bless African Americans with those things for themselves alone. God provided those blessings for the sake of others. Many African Americans with blessings from God forget where they got the blessings. Many forget that the purpose of their blessing is to help someone else. That is why many African Americans need to ask God for mercy.

We need to understand the healing mercies of God. However, there is no mercy without honesty. We need to be honest. Our nation needs to be honest. We must be honest as a people and honest as individuals. Honesty is the beginning of the mercy process. God needs to know that a person wants mercy. God has to know that a person is aware of his/her sins and weaknesses.

Before people ask one another for forgiveness, they need to ask God for forgiveness. It is God against whom they have sinned. It is not enough to ask for forgiveness. One must also forgive. Some African Americans have become more racist than white folks. Reacting to oppression, some African Americans become oppressive. For example, some African Americans classify one another as light skinned, dark skinned, and so forth. They react to one another differently based on skin color. Many with straight hair call their hair "good" hair, while those with kinky hair, call that "bad" hair. There is something wrong with

170

that. People who think this way need to ask God for forgiveness. God didn't give you big lips so they could be surgically reduced. God did not make junk. God made people the way they are.

If one is to experience the healing mercies of God, one must be honest. It is midnight in America. However, God is merciful. He continues to give America another chance. One of the former presidents said, "I tremble for this nation when I think that God is just." He must be hurt that the more He blesses America, the more America turns it back. How angry God must be to see what happened to Rodney King. America needs help.

America needs help that does not come from money or the president's office. America needs help from heaven. When God opens heaven, He can pour out so many blessings that no man or woman can count them. God wants to help. He wants to help America as a nation, and He wants to help individuals.

If you are reading this chapter and you are on dope, He'll help you. If you're old, evil and refusing to cooperate, He'll help you. If you're young and evil and caught up in a "hip hop" lifestyle, He'll help you. All you need to do is turn to God. He'll help you. He'll pick you up. He'll turn you around. He'll put your feet on a solid rock!

Pray with the psalmist: "Have mercy upon me O God, according to thy loving kindness: according to the multitude of thy tender mercies blot out my transgressions" (51:1). Hallejuah! Blot out my transgressions! There is something about the Lord that, no matter what sin you and I have committed, God's mercy can blot it out.

Therefore, the third point related to the healing power of God is that when one is honest and when God helps, then God sends His healing. David didn't know about the blood of Jesus. It is Jesus' blood that will blot out sins. Nothing can do this but the blood of Jesus. People are alive today, not because of how good they are, but because of the blood of Jesus. When I think of His goodness and what He's done for me, my soul gets happy.

It was His blood that woke us up this morning. It was His blood that put food on our table. It was His blood that provided us with education. It was His blood that allowed us to make it through many dangers, toils and snares. Let the blood fall on America, on the White House, on Congress, and on the State House. Let the blood fall on City Hall. Let it fall on dope addicts and prostitutes, and on the prisons. Let the blood of Jesus fall on me and you!

BIBLE STUDY APPLICATION

Instructions: Dr. Reid discussed the healing mercy of God throughout his sermon. The exercises below provide the opportunity to study God's mercy more closely. There are five exercises with six questions each. Then there is a church ministry application question and a personal application question.

1. The Mercy Seat

One of the most ancient symbols of God's mercy is the mercy seat. The mercy seat was at the very innermost and holiest place within the tabernacle. It was the lid of the Ark of the Covenant, the symbol of God's presence among the Israelites. God instructed the Israelites to construct it after they had sinned against Him by worshiping a golden calf.

a. Of what was the mercy seat made? (Exodus 25:17) With what is gold often associated? (Esther 1:5-7; 8:15; Job 23:10; Psalm 21:1-3; 45:9, 13)

b. What was constructed on each side of the mercy seat? (Exodus 25:17-20) When cherubim appear in Scripture, usually who is nearby? (Exodus 25:17-22; 26:1, 31; 1 Kings 6:23; 2 Kings 19:15; 1 Samuel 4:4; 2 Samuel 6:2; Psalm 80:1-2; 99:1)

c. What took place at the mercy seat? (Exodus 30:6; Leviticus 16:1-3)

172

d. What else took place at the mercy seat? (Leviticus 16:11-15; 1 Chronicles 28:11; Numbers 7:89)

e. Among Christians today what has taken the place of the mercy seat? (Hebrews 9:1-7; 10:11-23)

f. SUMMARY QUESTION: Suppose you were counseling someone who was imprisoned because of a sin they committed in the past. How would you use the information in questions a-e in encouraging them to come to Jesus?

2. Mercy and Forgiveness

God expresses His mercy by forgiving us of our sins.

a. What did God tell Moses about God's capacity to forgive? (Exodus 34:5-7) Of what importance were God's words for Moses's ministry among the Israelites? (Numbers 14:17-18)

b. What did God's promise of forgiveness mean to the Israelites at various points in their history? (Deuteronomy 13:12-17; Ezra 9:5-15; Psalm 6:1-10)

c. How did God express His mercy to the Gentiles? (Romans 11:25-36)

d. How did God express His mercy to Paul? (1 Corinthians 7:25; Acts 8:1-3; 9:1-16)

e. How has God shown His mercy to Christians? (Titus 3:1-8)

f. SUMMARY QUESTION: Suppose you have a pen pal who is afraid to join a church because of sins the person committed in the past. How would you use your answers to questions a-e to help the person?

3. Mercy and Covenant

God has expressed His mercy through covenants between Him and His people.

a. How did God express His mercy to Abraham? (Genesis 12:1-3; 15:1-7) How did He express His mercy to Moses? (Exodus 24:1-11; 34:28-32; 35:1-3) How did He express it

173

to David? (2 Samuel 7:12; 22:51)

b. Of what importance was God's covenantal mercy toward Solomon? (2 Chronicles 6:12-17) In what sense was God's covenant an expression of His mercy?

c. Of what importance was Nehemiah's memory of God's covenants? (Nehemiah 1:1-11) In what sense was Nehemiah's memory an expression of God's mercy?

d. Of what significance was the memory of God's covenants throughout the history of Israel? (Exodus 15:1-2, 13-18; 2 Samuel 7:1, 4-13; Psalm 25:6-10, 14-16) In what sense were these memories an expression of God's mercy?

e. What is the new covenant between the Lord and Christians today? (2 Corinthians 3:1-6; Hebrews 8:8-13) In what sense is it an expression of God's mercy?

f. SUMMARY QUESTION: Consider your answers to questions a-e. Are you in a covenant relationship with God? What is it? How is it an expression of God's mercy? Of what significance is the memory of God's goodness to you for your daily life?

4. God's Merciful Provisions

God has a history of expressing His mercy for us by providing for us and protecting us.

a. How did God show mercy to Joseph? (Genesis 39:1-23; 41:1-15, 37-46)

b. How does God show mercy to those who are poor? (Psalm 41)

c. How does God show mercy to those who are threatened by enemies? (Psalm 138)

d. How does God show mercy to those who are oppressed? (Psalm 123; 143; 144)

e. How does God show mercy to those who are sick? (Matthew 17:14-21; 20:29-34; Mark 10:46-52)

f. SUMMARY QUESTION: Do you know of anyone who is

in a situation similar to ones mentioned in questions a-e? How can you use the information to help them?

5. God's Eternal Love

God expresses His mercy by being eternally committed to us.

a. What is one sense in which God's love and mercy are eternal? (2 Samuel 22:36-51; 2 Chronicles 5:11-14)

b. What is another sense in which God's mercy is eternal? (Psalm 62)

c. What is the evidence that God's mercy is eternal? (Psalm 136)

d. What is another sense in which God's love and mercy are everlasting? (Psalm 23; Psalm 52)

e. What is yet another sense in which God's mercy is eternal? (Hebrews 4:14-16)

f. SUMMARY QUESTION: Is it possible to do anything that would cause God to refuse to hear your prayer for forgiveness or to honor your repentance? How can you use your answers to questions a-e to support your opinion?

6. CHURCH MINISTRY APPLICATION

Suppose you are involved with your church's prison ministry. How can you use the material in this chapter in encouraging people in prison to turn to Jesus? How can you use it to train people involved in the prison ministry? Outline a training course in prison ministry, using the contents of this chapter and other information you might have.

7. PERSONAL APPLICATION

Are you depressed because of a sin you have committed? How does this chapter relate to your situation? How can you apply what Dr. Reid wrote?

CHAPTER ELEVEN

A Voice in a Crisis

Often our professional lives distract us from our relationship with God. Sometimes we do not see how we can fit God into our busy schedules. Then, while we are attending to our careers, running our businesses, raising our children, keeping our husbands or wives happy, and "networking," a crisis abruptly enters our lives. Often the crisis forces us to the feet of Jesus, and opens us for a fresh touch from the Lord. Such is the story of Rev. Colleen Norman.

In the middle of a busy schedule which had distracted her from the church, the threat of malignant tumors abruptly entered her life. Facing the fact that the tumors could take her away from her husband and children forever, Rev. Norman came to Jesus for a fresh, healing touch, and He heard her cry. Her testimony is printed below. Following it is a sermon by Rev. Paul Sadler, entitled, "A Fresh Touch."

Eight years ago, when I was carrying my youngest daughter, gradually my voice began to change. I noticed that I became physically stronger than usual.

At first I didn't pay it any attention. I thought that perhaps I had a cold. However, as it went on for a few weeks, it got progressively worse. After a while, I could hardly talk. I thought I might have a virus. I was in my last trimester of pregnancy, so I ignored the symptoms.

The labor leading to the birth of my daughter was very difficult. Following her birth, other problems emerged. I noticed that it was difficult for my milk to come. Nursing the baby became excruciatingly painful. I decided to visit a doctor.

The doctor checked me and sent me to a gynecologist. The gynecologist was a brilliant African American woman, who took one look at me and told me that my hormones were out of order. She called my attention to symptoms of which I was completely unaware. For example, she asked me if I had noticed that I had begun to grow more body hair than usual, that a slight mustache was growing around my mouth, and that the hair was darker than usual. She thought that I might have a tumor somewhere. Among the possible locations were the base of my skull, my adrenal glands, my reproductive organs, or my liver. However, she said that the most likely place was my brain.

She asked me to return for tests in one month. After four days of tests, a tumor was found on my right ovary. It was certain that I would have to have it removed, and they were unsure as to whether it was malignant. The period of the tests, and the month of waiting that preceded them, was one of the most difficult periods of my life.

First there was the difficulty of discussing the situation with my family. I could only bring myself to share just so much with my husband or my mother-in-law from Alabama. I could not discuss it with my children. I recall the fear that I experienced during the tests. The doctors were telling me everything that they knew, but they continued to suspect something more than the test results were revealing. They discovered a tumor on my ovary, but they continued to suspect that there was more. This heightened the suspense and fear.

I had to deal with the fear, and I had to deal with the feeling

178

that my body was failing me. Then I had to deal with the notion of leaving my family. During the period of the tests, I had to face my personal mortality. I thought about leaving four children and a husband. I worried about whether my husband could raise my children by himself.

We even began to talk about a living will. We began talking about the funeral. In this crisis, my husband began to talk to me more. He became more honest and open. I was forced to have quality time with everyone. Everything looked different. My husband and I were forced to look at life as a whole. From whence did it come? Could I ever become healthy and whole? If not, where would I like to be? What would I do with the time I had remaining? After a while, I found that I could only share so much with any human being. Then I knew that I could only talk with God. It was in this crisis that my entire relationship with God changed.

Before this crisis, I had a distant relationship with God. I had been raised in church. I was a church member, officially, but I had not been attending regularly. I had been raised in the Pentecostal church and then had converted to Catholicism. However, as my family became more successful, the church seemed less and less important. It was certainly not my primary focus. In fact, our family was facing the difficulty of debt, and I really didn't want to be pregnant again. I had become angry with God and frustrated, wondering if God was going to work things out for us, or if things were just going to happen.

I had stopped praying and going to church. However, the night before my surgery, when they were to remove the tumor from my ovary in order to test it, I came face to face with the Lord. I had gone to bed, but I woke up after two hours. My family was asleep. I walked into the family room, sat down and cried. For the first time in a long time, I prayed. I asked the Lord for strength. Then I heard the Lord speak.

It was not audible. It was more like a thought intruding upon my thoughts. A voice came and interrupted me. It was a voice which one does not confuse with any other voice. It was unique and it was distinguished. The Lord told me that it was going to be all right, and that He would be with my family. It was just that distinct.

Calmness filled me. I sat there for a while, because I didn't want to lose this experience. However, I didn't lose it. He has been with me every day since then.

On the following day, they removed the tumor and ran tests on it. The doctors ran the tests three times and discovered that the tumor was benign.

Since that time, I have come to see life differently. There have been many developments in my life with the Lord. He has called me into the Christian ministry, and within months I will complete my seminary training at Chicago Theological Seminary. My little daughter is now eight years old. I am a part of the praise team at Trinity United Church of Christ in Chicago, and my entire family belongs to the church.

Rev. Colleen Norman

A FRESH TOUCH

Rev. Paul H. Sadler
Psalm 80

Do you ever feel like something is missing in your life? Perhaps the joy that you once had is gone or perhaps you've never had any real joy. Perhaps you come to church Sunday after Sunday and go away feeling empty and void. Perhaps there is no fulfillment in work and no happiness at play. Do you develop relationships that remain superficial because you are not happy with yourself?

Perhaps things aren't going right in your marriage. Perhaps your wife doesn't understand you or your husband is insensitive to your needs. Perhaps your children are all grown and the sound of emptiness in your home has become more than you can bear. Retirement may have left a void in your life, and perhaps the so-called leisure time cannot replace the fulfillment you once received from working in your chosen profession.

As you read this chapter do you feel that something is missing in your life? Has sickness in your body or in a family member's body left you discouraged? If any of these questions apply to you, then perhaps you need a fresh touch. If so, Psalm 80 has a word for you. Verse 17 says, "Let thy hand be upon the man of thy right hand, upon the son of man whom thou madest strong for thyself" (Psalm 80:17, KJV).

The touch of the hand has always had power and significance. Touches of hands have many meanings. We touch to greet. We touch in parting. We touch in loving. We touch in scolding. We touch in fighting. We touch in teaching. We touch in healing. We touch in building. We touch in confronting, and we touch in rejoicing. Each of these touches has a different meaning. In the church, the laying on of hands signifies the imparting of the Spirit of God. We lay on hands to bless. We lay on hands to baptize. We lay on hands to confirm. We lay on hands to ordain. For every act of life, the touch of the hand has power and significance.

In Psalm 80 the Children of Israel ask God to lay hands on them as God's chosen people. Even the people of God need a fresh touch sometimes. The Israelites had suffered emptiness in life without God. They were similar to God's people today.

Every morning Christians should wake up, fall on their knees, lie on the bed (if one must), or stand and thank God. After thanking God for the previous night's sleep, and for that morning's rising, one needs to ask the Lord for a fresh touch. Follow the example of our foreparents who said, "Father, I stretch my hand to thee. No other help I know. If thou withdraw thyself from me, whither shall I go?"

After working hard all week, and giving one's best to the Master, with some successes and some failures, some ups and some downs, some good moments and some bad ones, most Christians need a fresh touch from the hand of God.

In Psalm 80, the Israelites indicated that they needed that touch. They even sang about it. In verse 18, they sang about their request and about the anticipated results of the expected answer to their prayers. In other words, the psalmist said, "Lord, with Your hand on our shoulder we can't turn back any more. Revive us and we will sing Your praise! Revive us and we will preach the Gospel! Revive us and we will teach Your Word! Revive us and we will serve Your people! Revive us and we will feed the hungry, clothe the naked, and house the homeless! Revive us and we will call on Your name! We will offer You no more meaningless messages, no more spiritless songs, no more pitiful prayers, and no more cold, dead worship services!"

When a person approaches the Lord as the Children of Israel approached God, s/he is asking for a fresh touch from God. When a person feels the touch of the Lord, that touch will make a difference in his/her life. The person doesn't have to jump over any pews but if a person's religion doesn't make him/her feel good, then something is still missing. That person still needs a fresh touch!

Let's examine Psalm 80 a little more closely, particularly the refrain in verse 19: "Turn us again, O Lord God of hosts, cause thy face to shine; and we shall be saved." In conclusion, remember three major points.

First of all, every Christian needs a fresh touch sometimes. A Christian shouldn't be afraid to ask for special prayer. Prayer changes things! A Christian shouldn't be ashamed to cry. Tears are the flood gates of the emotions. Release them and let the waters flow!

By way of a personal testimony, I have thrown away more dignity than most people have ever had and all that dignity is not worth five sticks of chewing gum. There is no middle ground for God's church. God's people will either die with their own private dignity or they will live with God's joy! However, a Christian cannot get that joy without a fresh touch from God. Every Christian needs a fresh touch sometimes!

Secondly, please remember that when God blesses a life with God's touch, that person will need to thank God! There are many ways to thank God for His goodness. Like the psalmist, one can thank God by calling His name. One can thank God by bringing tithes and offerings into His storehouse. One can thank God by working and serving in the church. One can thank God by witnessing and bringing souls into the house of faith. When God blesses a person's life with His touch, that person needs to thank God.

Thirdly, remember that Psalm 80 tells us that one is not saved by what one does, one is saved by what God did. In verse 19 the psalmist asks God to make God's face to shine upon the Children of Israel that they may be saved. The question is, what did the psalmist and the Israelites sense that was missing? What was the missing piece? Many of us feel that a piece is missing from our lives.

When God created humans, He left a piece missing. However, the missing piece is readily available. Nearly two thousand years ago God sent that missing piece. That piece (or peace) was a small child born in a stable. By the time He was two years old, He had been exiled from His homeland. At the age of 12, He reasoned with the elders in the temple. As an adult, He explained the way to salvation, the way to locate the missing piece! But people didn't understand Him, the missing peace. At the appointed time, they delivered Him into the hands of the enemy and they crucified Him on Calvary. They crucified the missing piece.

However, God would not allow the disbelief of a few to block that missing piece from access to all of creation. That is why one

Sunday morning He got up from the grave and gave that peace to everyone who would call on His name. Since that day, if anyone needs a fresh touch from God, a person can get it! If a person needs salvation, the person can come to Jesus. If there is a missing peace in your life, come to Jesus today!

BIBLE STUDY APPLICATION

Instructions: Rev. Sadler mentioned that everyone needs a special touch from the Lord. In the Bible, special touches of the Lord came in the form of special anointing for ministry, and daily fresh touches of the Holy Spirit. The exercises below provide the opportunity to study some of these fresh touches more closely. There are five exercises, with six questions each. Then there is a church ministry application question and a personal application question.

1. God Touches Saul

Rev. Sadler mentioned that Christians need a special touch from the Lord for service. God touched (or anointed) Saul for special Christian service.

a. Who was Saul? (1 Samuel 9:12, 15-17, 21-27; 10:1)

b. What was the situation among the Children of Israel when Saul was to become king? (1 Samuel 8:1-22)

c. In his natural flesh, how did Saul feel about becoming king? (1 Samuel 10:17-23)

d. Why did Saul need a special touch (or anointing) for service? (1 Samuel 10:1, 9-13)

e. To what ancient tradition did Saul's special touch relate? (Exodus 30:22-33; Numbers 27:12-23)

f. SUMMARY QUESTION: Compare and contrast Saul's special touch with the fresh touch to which Rev. Sadler refers. How is it similar? How is it different? In what ways

184

is Saul's situation similar to yours?

2. God Touches David

God also provided a special touch or anointing for David.

a. Who was David? (1 Samuel 16:1, 4-13)

b. What was the situation in Israel when David became king? (1 Samuel 15:10-29)

c. What stresses did David's new job bring? (1 Samuel 18:6-16; 19:1)

d. In what sense did David's anointing occur over and over again? (Psalm 23)

e. What role did the fresh touches of the Holy Spirit play in David's life?

f. SUMMARY QUESTION: Compare and contrast David's fresh touches with those mentioned by Rev. Sadler. How are they similar? How are they different? In what ways is David's situation similar to yours?

3. God Touches Solomon

God also provided a special anointing for Solomon.

a. Who was Solomon? (2 Samuel 12:24-25; 1 Kings 1:32-35)

b. What were the conditions in Israel when Solomon became king? (1 Kings 1:1-27, 49-53)

c. In what sense did Solomon realize that he always needed a fresh touch from the Lord? (1 Kings 3:1-9)

d. How did the Lord respond to Solomon's request for a fresh touch? (1 Kings 3:10-15)

e. What was the outcome of Solomon's touch from the Lord? (1 Kings 4:20-34)

f. SUMMARY QUESTION: Compare and contrast Saul's anointing with those mentioned by Rev. Sadler. How was it different? How was it similar?

185

4. Jesus and a Fresh Touch

Jesus realized that He also needed a daily fresh touch from His heavenly Father.

a. What is one time that Jesus received a special touch? (Matthew 3:13-17)

b. What is a time when Jesus needed a fresh touch? (Matthew 4:1-11)

c. What is another time that Jesus realized that He needed a fresh touch? (Mark 6:45-47; Matthew 14:13)

d. What is yet another time that Jesus realized that He needed a fresh touch? (Matthew 26:36-46; Mark 14:32-42; Luke 22:39-46)

e. What is yet another time that Jesus realized that He needed a fresh touch? (Mark 15:33-41; Luke 23:44-49; John 19:28-30)

f. SUMMARY QUESTION: Compare and contrast Jesus' need for a fresh touch with times in your life when you have needed a fresh touch, in the course of your ministry.

5. Fresh Touches in the Book of Acts

After the death, burial, resurrection and ascension of Christ, the disciples needed a special touch in order to carry out Jesus' ministry on earth.

a. What circumstances surrounded the apostles' need for a special touch from the Lord? (Acts 1:12--2:4)

b. What is a circumstance in which believers realized that they needed a fresh touch? (Acts 4:23-31)

c. Why did the Ethiopian eunuch feel that he needed a special touch from the Lord? (Acts 8:26-40)

d. When did Peter need a fresh touch? (Acts 12:1-19)

e. When did Stephen need a fresh touch? (Acts 7:54-60)

f. SUMMARY QUESTION: Compare and contrast your answers to questions a-e. What are the similarities and differences between all of these people who needed a fresh touch? How are they different and similar to people who need a fresh touch today?

6. CHURCH MINISTRY APPLICATION

Consider people in the various ministries of your church. Then recall some of your answers to exercises 1-5. Are there ways that your church can implement special programs and events where such people can receive special prayers and opportunities for fresh touches?

7. PERSONAL APPLICATION

Do you need a fresh touch from the Lord? Review Rev. Sadler's sermon and Rev. Norman's testimony. Then seek the Lord for a fresh touch.

CHAPTER TWELVE

Art of Survival

Many of us expect that the country in which we live is always going to be healthy. We take it for granted that the economy will always provide us with a job, or with government assistance until we are able to locate one. We take it for granted that we will be able to survive, by the skill of our minds, hands or muscles. Therefore, we place our faith in ourselves and in our government. However, Rev. Ace Ware learned that survival from day to day (national or personal) could not be taken for granted. Rev. Ware lived through the disaster of the Great Depression of the 1930s.

He was a young boy, living in Chicago when the stock market crashed. He tells the story of how God's hand guided his life and the lives of members of his family, as they rose above those circumstances. His testimony is printed below. Following it is a sermon by Bishop Charles Blake, on rising above circumstances.

My story is the story of how God guided my life, taking me to places where I had never been, and leading me to places where I did not know that I was going. It was His invisible but ever-present hand that drew me to the right places at the right time, and prepared me for the ministry to which He would later call me.

My mother and father had separated when I was an infant, during the 1920s, before the Great Depression. I never knew my father until much later in my life, in the 1940s, after I was a grown man. However, I was only six years old when my mother brought me to Chicago. It was in 1927, just two years prior to the famous stock market crash that would result in the Depression of the 1930s.

In those days, African Americans worked for stock yards, railroads, and foundries. However, my mother was a very talented artist. She designed lamp shades in various ornate designs. She had a job in a shop. She would bring some of the leftover lamp shades home, and we would all admire her work.

While we were in Chicago, my mother met and married a good man, who became a minister in his later years. He also had a business. He was an ice man. He kept a horse in a stable and a wagon in back of our home. My mother and stepfather took care of the horses. I recall that we moved around quite a bit, but for a while, my mother and stepfather lived upstairs, and I lived downstairs with my grandmother.

I remember that we had more money than most African American families that I knew during those times. For example, we were the only family we knew that had a radio and a phonograph. My family always took me to church. We attended Zion Hill Baptist Church. My mother sang in the choir there, and I attended Sunday School. From a very young age, I began to sense that the Lord had a special claim on my life.

We were doing very well until, when I was about 10 years old, my mother died. She had gone into the hospital twice, but after the second time, she died. My stepfather sold the furniture in the house and left me with my grandmother. It was during the middle of the Depression, right after my mother died, that my entire life changed. We were plunged into a type of poverty that

I had never known before. My grandmother had the challenge of supporting me, along with her other two children, who were teenagers.

My grandmother was about 45 years old at the time. She had lived in the South for most of her life, and she was not accustomed to the big city life of Chicago. My grandmother continued to go to church, and we became dependent on relief from the government.

One thing that stands out from the pain of those days, is the vision of myself as a young boy, not having very many clothes, and almost always wearing worn shoes, sometimes with holes in them. However, in the midst of that, I also remember hearing the still small voice of God, speaking to me from time to time. It was so real that it almost made me uncomfortable.

I also remember that there were very few African Americans living on the West Side of Chicago where we lived. I recall that most of the teachers were Irish, the firemen were Irish, and the policemen were all Irish. I never saw Black people in those roles. The people who drove the buses were mostly Irish. Therefore, it was not normal for a Black child to aspire to any of those positions. Most African Americans in Chicago at the time expected to be discriminated against in almost any job other than the foundries, railroads and coal yards.

When my soul looks back on this, I realize that there is only one way that I got over. It was only by the grace of God. In those days, we worked together as a family for survival, and God provided the jobs. My aunt, who was about 16 years old at the time, got a job doing housework. My uncle, who was about 19 at the time, got a job working in an automobile garage. They helped to pay our bills with those jobs, whenever they could get them. I remember that the Irish teachers at my school took up a collection when it was time for me to graduate. With that collection, they bought me graduation clothing. That, too, was the grace of God.

After high school, I got a job digging ditches. However, I was gifted in art work. In those days, most young Black children did not think about how they could use artistic skills in careers. They didn't expect those careers to be available to them, and usually they were not. Most Blacks did not work in those fields in Chicago of that time. However, the Lord made a way for me.

It happened one day when a social worker came to my grandmother's house. She noticed my art work and asked who was responsible for it. Then the social worker came back and gave me a note, inviting me to apply for a position in the Arts Project of what was the Works Program Administration (WPA). It was a federal program designed to help young people get jobs. That was nothing but the grace of God.

In my new job, I did the layouts for posters. My posters announced artists who were coming to town to perform at places like Grant Park and the Music Hall. I can recall making posters for such giants as Marian Anderson and Paul Robeson. In that job, I met many famous people.

Who would ever have expected a young teenager, who did not have enough money to purchase graduation clothes, to meet such famous people as Richard Wright, Studs Terkel and Charles White? All of them were working in the WPA program around the same time I was. I did not realize who these people were until they had become famous, many years later.

Later, I worked at the University of Chicago in metallurgy. I remained there until I retired. In that job, I learned how to analyze chemicals in the air using a mass spectrometer. My entire occupational path was directed by God. However, that was not all there was. God was not finished with me yet.

At the age of about 28, I was called to the ministry. I remember sitting in the back of the sanctuary at the Church of God in Christ when Elder Walker was preaching. I glanced around at the profiles of people, and then looked up at the minister. Suddenly people appeared like little birds, and the minister appeared like a mother bird, feeding her young. In a still small voice, the Lord spoke to me and told me that He wanted me to feed the children of God.

God's call to the ministry was affirmed by others. For example, one night when I went to the north side of Chicago to hear a minister speak, a very unusual thing happened. The minister was a white woman. She had great spiritual insight. She kept looking at me. Then she said that she wanted me to come up to the front. She called out, "What are you waiting for? God has called you to the ministry!" From that night on, I felt more and more that the Lord had called me to ministry.

Today I am the associate minister at Evangelistic Crusaders Church of God in Christ. I have been at this church for 20 years. When my soul looks back and wonders, I have no doubt in my mind how I got over!

Rev. Ace Ware

RISING ABOVE CIRCUMSTANCES!

Bishop Charles Blake
Psalm 18

One of the most important human abilities is the ability to rise above circumstances and emotions. People who can rise above circumstances have a great chance for success. People who cannot are doomed to failure and sorrow.

Let's first take a look at circumstances. People often predict the future based on current circumstances. In other words, circumstances are usually the criteria for gauging chances for success. Sometimes an automatic excuse for failure is the phrase, "circumstances beyond our control."

Many are more intent on changing their circumstances than on changing themselves. For them, circumstances are primary. Every day people tell pastors, "If only I could live in a different time. If only I had a different pastor. If I could just go to a different church, or live in a different house, or in a different apartment. I need to get away from my family," they say. "My wife is dragging me down," or "I have a no good husband. I'm tired of my neighborhood. I'm tired of my job. I just need a change."

However, the same circumstances that will destroy one person will make another person great. That is why enemies surround us with unpleasantness and pain. But most of our circumstances are mild when compared to those of David.

However, God can change your circumstances. If God does not change your circumstances, God can change you in the midst of them, so that you can rise above them.

In David's case, he had to deal both with adverse circumstances and with related unpleasant emotions. David said that floods of ungodly men had him afraid (Psalm 18:4). The first emotion he had to deal with was fear. Fear grips many people today. People are fearful regarding their marriages. People are fearful regarding their jobs, social relationships, personal welfare and safety. Many are afraid but don't know they are afraid. Fear is painful.

In addition to fear, David had to deal with the emotion of sorrow--sorrow related to death. Sorrow is another name for depression. Sorrow and depression are today's national epidemics.

The third emotion that David was experiencing was distress. Distress can be either a circumstance or an emotion. As a circumstance, it came to David in the form of trouble. As an emotion, it came to David in the form of a feeling. David listed his emotions as sorrow, fear, and distress.

However, David looked away from his circumstances to the almighty God. David had a concept of who God was and what God could do. In three short verses, David called God ten different names. In verse two, David says God is the Creator, the Ruler of the universe. David knew that God could fix anything He had made. David knew that God could control anything He had made.

David was like the little girl on the rushing, roaring train that seemed almost out of control. The little girl was playing with her doll. Someone asked the little girl, "Aren't you afraid?" She said, "Oh no, my father is the engineer of this train and he knows I'm on the train." In other words, our Father is the Creator of the universe, and He knows we are here. In Psalm 18:1, David refers to God as his personal Master. He says that God is in control of his life. David knew that when God is Master and when we are His servants, we don't have to worry about anything. God will take care of His own.

If God owns something, He will take care of it. "Be not dismayed whatever betide, God will take care of you!"[1]

David also called God his strength. He says, "I will love thee, oh Lord, my strength" (Psalm 18:1). It is important to know the source of one's strength. The psalmist said, "My help is in the name of the Lord. God is my refuge and my strength, a very present help in trouble. It is in Him that we live and that we move and that we have our being" (Psalm 46:1). Strength is not in wisdom, wealth, intelligence, or ability. Strength is in God. If God withdrew His hand for one moment, it would all be over.

Then in Psalm 18:2, David says that the Lord is his rock. "If a person wants a house to stand, the person should build the house on a rock, not on sand!" (Matthew 7:24) "Remember, time is filled with swift transitions. Naught on earth unmoved shall stand. Build your hopes on things eternal, and hold to God's unchanging hand."[2] One song writer said, "On Christ the solid rock I stand. All other ground is sinking sand."[3] David said, "I've got a rock that I can stand on. When my heart is overwhelmed lead me to the rock that he higher than I."

Then David called the Lord his fortress. Remember in the old cowboy and Indian movies, when the cowboys would hide inside the fort? Remember how the Indians would shoot their fiery arrows and then get on their ladders and climb over the walls of the fort? That's not the type of fortress that the psalmist was talking about. David said, "The Lord is my fortress" (v. 2).

195

When the Lord is your fortress, your enemies can't get over Him. They can't get around Him. They can't get under Him. You can sit down on the inside, cross your legs, fold your arms, look at television, and relax, because the Lord is your fortress!

David says that the Lord is also his deliverer. Whoever the Son sets free, is free indeed. Where the Spirit of God is, there is liberty (2 Corinthians 3:17). It doesn't matter what type of program you are on, the Lord can set you free. The Lord can deliver you.

Then David said God was his buckler. A buckler is a shield. A shield protects a person from rocks, arrows, darts, bullets and words. When a person holds a shield, the person's safety depends on keeping the shield between the person and the enemy. However, when the Lord is the shield, He is a shield around, above and underneath the person. The enemy cannot get to you.

David says the Lord is the horn of his salvation! The horn is a symbol of power and strength. David went on to say that the Lord is his high tower! When the storms of life are raging, you have a high tower that you can enter and rise above everything that enemies try to do to you. They may talk about you, but you'll rise above it. They may try to hinder you, but you'll rise above them. They may try to drag you down, but you will rise above them. Temptations may come, but you will rise above them. Trials will come, but you will be above them, because you will be in the high tower of the Lord!

Then last but not least, David says the Lord is worthy to be praised. People praise many people who are not worthy to be praised, but God is worthy to be praised.

David knew who his God was and what his God was like. Then he knew what he was going to do. He had four ways to overcome his circumstances and emotions. First he said, "I will love the Lord" (Psalm 18:1). David made a conscious decision to love God because God is God.

The Bible says, "Seek ye first the kingdom of God, and his righteousness; and all these things shall be added unto you" (Matthew 6:33, KJV). If you love God, you will please God. You will obey Him. You will want to be around Him. You will call on Him. You will walk in His way.

David also made the conscious decision to trust in the Lord. He didn't trust in circumstances or emotions. The Bible says, "Trust in the Lord with all thine heart; and lean not to thine own understanding. In all thy ways acknowledge him, and He shall direct thy paths" (Proverbs 3:5-6, KJV).

David said he would love God, trust God and call on God. To call on God is to refuse to rely on other resources. To call on God is to let God know that He is the source from whom your blessings flow. To call on God is to proclaim your faith. To call on God is to focus your being on God Himself.

The Bible says, "Call unto me, and I will answer thee, and show thee great and mighty things, which thou knowest not" (Jeremiah 33:3, KJV). Call God when you're in trouble. Call Him when you're in distress. Call Him when there is trouble all around you. David said, "In my distress I called upon the Lord, and cried unto my God: he heard my voice out of his temple" (Psalm 18:6). The Bible says, "You have not because you ask not" (James 4:2). "Ask and it shall be given. Seek and ye shall find. Knock and it shall be opened" (Matthew 7:7). "Oh what peace we often forfeit! Oh what needless pains we bear! All because we do not carry, everything to God in prayer!"[4]

David knew that if he loved, trusted, and called upon the Lord, he would be saved. The song says be not dismayed whatever be tide. God will take care of you.[5]

However, David was doing more than just saying that God was going to save him. David was saying that he had decided that he was going to make it. He said he was not going to lose. He was going to overcome.

As you read the final paragraph of this chapter, you need to decide that you will not allow earthly circumstances to pull you down. You need to decide not to allow mistakes from the past to hold you back. You need to decide not to allow people who hate you to hinder you. Decide that you are going to make it.

Think about Christ in you. The hope of glory. Say, "My heart is fixed. My mind is made up. Lightning may flash, storms may roll, floods may rise, but I'm going to make it in the name of the Lord!" God is calling for you to love Him, trust Him, and call on Him. I wish that I could lay hands on every person reading this chapter. However, I realize that the hand of the Lord is already upon you, delivering you and setting you free. Praise the Lord! The Lord is blessing you right now!

BIBLE STUDY APPLICATION

Instructions: Dr. Blake said that one of the most important human abilities is the ability to rise above circumstances. David the psalmist was able to do this. The exercises here provide the opportunity to study the life of David more closely, and to learn how he rose above circumstances. There are five exercises, with six questions each. Then there is a church ministry application question and a personal application question.

1. Rising Above Life as a Shepherd (1 Samuel 16:1; Psalm 23)

David was born into some very rough circumstances. He had to assume an enormous amount of responsibility as a child. Yet he was able to reach out to the Lord, and then rise above his circumstances.

a. What responsibilities did the child David have? (1 Samuel 17:31-32, 12-15)

b. What did shepherds do in the morning? (John 10:1-5)

c. What did shepherds do in the evening? (Jeremiah 33:12-13; Ezekiel 20:37)

d. What did shepherds do at night? (Luke 2:8; Nahum 3:18)

e. How did David rise above his circumstances as a shepherd? (Psalm 23)

f. SUMMARY QUESTION: Into what types of rough circumstances are many African American children thrust today? In what ways are many of them forced to function as adults, while still children? How can Psalm 18 and Psalm 23 be used to help such children rise above their circumstances? Which specific verses apply?

2. Rising Above Goliaths (1 Samuel 16 & 17)

It must have been a difficult circumstance for David to stand before a menacing giant. Yet memories of God's goodness gave him courage to overcome this threat.

a. How did it come about that David was in Saul's court? (1 Samuel 16:14-23)

b. What was the threat that the Israelites faced? (1 Samuel 17:1-11, 16)

c. How did David become exposed to what was threatening the Israelites? (1 Samuel 17:17-25)

d. What was David's attitude toward Goliath? (1 Samuel 17:26-29) Where did he get such an attitude? (17:34-40)

e. How did David rise above his circumstances? (1 Samuel 17:41-54) How did his attitude about God help him?

f. SUMMARY QUESTION: Symbolically speaking, what are some "Goliaths" that African Americans face today? What are some "Goliaths" in your life? What steps should you follow in conquering your personal "Goliath?" How does Psalm 1 apply?

3. Rising Above Envious Enemies (1 Samuel 1:15-16; 19:1, 8--20:1)

Some people hate to see others succeed. They automatically become envious and attempt to hurt the successful person or block his/her success. David became the victim of such an envious person. Yet with God, he rose above this circumstance.

a. Who was envious of David and why? (1 Samuel 18:15-16; 19:1)

b. The more successful David became, what happened? (1 Samuel 18:30; 19:8-12)

c. What were some supportive relationships that the Lord provided for David? How did David make use of them? (1 Samuel 19:1-7, 11-18; 20:1-4; 21:1-6) How did they help him to rise above circumstances? What can you learn from this?

d. What was the main support that David sought, and from whom? (1 Samuel 23:1-2; 24:1-14) What can you learn from this?

e. What was the outcome of David's struggle against his enemies? (1 Samuel 31:1-11) Emotionally speaking, how did God help David rise above his circumstances? (2 Samuel 1:1-2, 11-27) What can you learn from this?

f. SUMMARY QUESTION: Do you have enemies? What are they trying to do to you? Reread Psalm 18. How can the Lord help you rise above threats from your enemies? How can you rise above the threats they impose on you? What can you learn from David's situation?

4. Dealing with Personal Flaws and Limitations (2 Samuel 11)

Because we are human, we are not perfect. Often the weaknesses of our human nature cause us to do wrong to ourselves and others. The knowledge of our own wrongdoing is a very difficult circumstance to confront. David found himself in this circumstance. Yet, with God's help, he was able to admit his wrongdoing, seek forgiveness and continue with the remainder of his life.

a. What took place between David and Bathsheba? (2 Samuel 11:1-5, 14-17, 26-27)

b. What took place between David and Uriah, Bathsheba's husband? (2 Samuel 11:6-17)

c. What was wrong with what David did? (Leviticus 18:19-20; Malachi 3:5; Job 24:13-17; Proverbs 5:15-20)

d. What was the traditional punishment for what David had done? (Leviticus 20:10; Deuteronomy 22:22) What was David's punishment? (2 Samuel 12:1-15)

e. What evidence is there that David confessed and repented for his sins? (2 Samuel 12:13)

f. SUMMARY QUESTION: Have you ever become aware of your personal inadequacies and limitations? Have you ever hurt someone in a way that you regret? How can you use David's example discussed in questions a-e, to rise above this circumstance?

5. Dealing with Difficult Children

Sometimes serious conflicts develop between parents and their children. Sometimes the personal limitations of parents pass onto their children. Sometimes one is unable to save a difficult child from an untimely death. When one is in the midst of such a crisis, it is difficult to visualize a way out of the crisis. David found himself in such a situation.

a. Who was Absalom, and what were the circumstances into which he was born? (2 Samuel 13--14) How might this have affected his early life?

b. What happened early in Absalom's life? (2 Samuel 13:1-22)

c. What type of relationship did Absalom have with his father, and how might that have affected him as he was growing up? (2 Samuel 13:23-27) What personal limitations did David seem to have?

d. What type of relationship eventually developed between David and Absalom? (2 Samuel 13:24-27) What was the eventual outcome? (2 Samuel 19:11-31; 18:1-12)

e. How did the Lord help David rise above the difficult circumstance of losing a difficult son? (2 Samuel 18:33; Psalm 18) What specific verses best apply?

f. SUMMARY QUESTION: Difficult relationships between parents, sons and daughters are not new. Are you or one of your relatives in such a circumstance? What can you learn from David's situation? Does Dr. Blake's chapter offer any insights?

6. CHURCH MINISTRY APPLICATION

Does your church offer opportunities for fathers, mothers and their children to communicate and solve conflicts? Which ministries in your church could develop a program to help parents and young people with this type of challenge? What would be the design of it? How might both saved and unsaved people participate and benefit, or do you believe that is possible?

7. PERSONAL APPLICATION

Are you in a difficult circumstance? What can you learn from David's life that may help you? What parts of Psalm 18 already apply to your life? What do you have that David did not have? Can you apply any insights from Dr. Blake's sermon?

FOOTNOTES

Introduction

1. Townsend, A.M., *The Baptist Standard Hymnal* (Nashville: Townsend Press, Sunday School Board, National Baptist Convention USA, Inc., 1985), p. 700.

2. Diop, Cheikh Anta, *The African Origin of Civilization: Myth or Reality*, translated by Mercer Cook (Chicago: Lawrence Hill Books, 1974), p. 179.

3. Blassingame, John W., *Slave Testimony* (Baton Rouge: Louisiana State University Press).

4. Harding, Vincent, *There Is a River* (New York: Vintage Books, 1983).

5. Raboteau, Albert J., *Slave Religion* (New York: Oxford University, 1980).

6. Asante, Molefi K. and Mark T. Mattson, *The Historical and Cultural Atlas of African Americans* (New York: MacMillin, 1992).

7. Foster, William Z., *The Negro People in American History* (New York: International Publishers, 1954).

8. Asante and Mattson, p. 3.

9. Asante and Mattson, p. 26.

10. Asante and Mattson, p. 26.

11. Harding, p. 16.

12. Asante and Mattson, p. 27.

13. Asante and Mattson, p. 39.

14. Asante and Mattson, p. 50.

15. Raboteau, p. 213.

16. Raboteau, p. 214.

17. Raboteau, p. 212.

18. Raboteau, p. 219.

19. Raboteau, p. 217.

20. Raboteau, p. 218.

21. Raboteau, p. 214.

22. Raboteau, p. 226.

23. Raboteau, p. 227.

24. Asante and Mattson, p. 39.

25. Asante and Mattson, p. 186.

26. Foster, p. 162.

27. Blassingame, p. 111.

28. Blassingame, p. 112.

29. Blassingame, pp. 22-23.

30. Blassingame, pp. 22-23.

31. Blassingame, p. 18.

32. Blassingame, pp. 5-7.

33. Blassingame, p. 19.

34. Blassingame, pp. 91-92.

35. Blassingame, pp. 114-115.

36. Blassingame, pp. 93-95.

37. Blassingame, pp. 98-108.

38. Wilmore, G. *Black Religion and Black Radicalism* (New York: Orbis Books, 1990), pp. 39, 79, 96.

Chapter Five

Hughes, Langston and Arna Bontemps, *The Poetry of the Negro 1746-1970* (New York: Doubleday & Co., 1970), p. 53.

Chapter Seven

1. Trueblood, Elton, *Abraham Lincoln: Theologian of American Anguish* (New York: Harper and Row, 1973), p. 8.

2. Finkelstein, Louis, ed., *American Autobiographies, Fifteen Self-Portraits* (New York: Harper, 1948), p. 183.

3. "The Loneliness of Christ," *Sermons Preached at Brighton* (New York: Harper and Brothers, n.d.), p. 177.

Chapter Nine

1. *The New National Baptist Hymnal* (Nashville: National Baptist Publishing Board, 1977), p. 162.

Chapter Twelve

1. *The New National Baptist Hymnal* (Nashville: National Baptist Publishing Board, 1977), p. 220.

2. *The New National Baptist Hymnal,* p. 248.

3. *The New National Baptist Hymnal,* p. 223.
4. *The New National Baptist Hymnal,* p. 340.
5. *The New National Baptist Hymnal,* p. 220.

BIBLIOGRAPHY

Austin, Allan D. *African Muslims in Antebellum America: A Sourcebook* New York: Garland, 1984.

Barrow, Willie, "The Black Church as Agent of Social Change: The Harold Washington Story" in *The Black Church and the Harold Washington Story*. Bristol: Wyndham Hall Press, 1988.

Bartchy, S. Scott. *First Century Slavery and 1 Corinthians 7:21*. Missoula, Montana: Scholar's Press, 1973.

Bennett, G. Willis. *Effective Urban Church Ministry*. Nashville: Broadman Press, 1983.

Berry, Mary, and John Blassingame. *Long Memory: The Black Experience in America*. New York: Oxford University Press, 1982.

Blassingame, John. *The Slave Community: Plantation Life in the Antebellum South*. New York: Oxford University Press, 1972.

Black New Orleans, 1860-1880. Chicago: University of Chicago Press, 1973.

Brinson, Sylvester, III. "Harold Washington: A Champion of Hope" in *The Black Church and the Harold Washington Story*. Bristol: Wyndham Hall Press, 1988.

Byers, David M., and Quinn Bernard. *New Directions for the Rural Church*. New York: Paulist, 1978.

Clarke, John Henrik. *African World Revolution*. Trenton: African World Press, Inc., 1991.

Cleage, Albert. *The Black Messiah*. Fairway, Kansas: Andrews & McMeel Inc., 1969.

Cole, Johnnetta B. "The Cultural Base in Education" in *Infusion of African and African American Content in the School Curriculum* edited by Asa Hilliard III, Lucretia Payton-Stewart and Larry Obadele Williams. Morristown: Aaron Press, 1990.

Coleman, D.C. "Harold Washington as a Role Model for Black Youth" in *The Black Church and the Harold Washington Story*. Bristol: Wyndham Hall Press, 1988.

Collier-Thomas, Bettye. *Black Women in America: Contributors to Our Heritage*. Washington, D.C.: Bethune Museum-Archives, 1983.

Cone, James H. *A Black Theology of Liberation*. Philadelphia: Lippincott, 1970.

Cooper, Anna Julia. *A Voice from the South: By a Black Woman of the South*.

Kenia, Ohio: Aldine Publishing, 1892.

Copher, Charles. "Bible Characteristics, Events, Places and Images Remembered and Celebrated in Black Worship." *The Journal of Interdemonational Theological Seminary*. Fall, 1986, Spring, 1987, pp. 75-86.

Cotton, Jesse. "The Role of the Clergy in the Harold Washington Story" in *The Black Church and the Harold Washington Story*. Bristol: Wyndham Hall Press, 1988.

Curtin, Phillip. *The Atlantic Slave Trade*. Madison: University of Wisconsin Press, 1969.

Davis, Allison, and John Dollard. *Children of Bondage: The Personality Development of Negro Youth in the Urban South*. Washington, D.C.: American Council on Education, 1940.

Dodson, Jualynne. "Nineteenth Century A.M.E. Preaching Women." Hilah F. Thomas and Rosemary Skinner Keller, editors. *Women in New Worlds*. Nashville: Abingdon, 1981, pp. 276-89.

Drake, St. Clair, and Horace Cayton. *Black Metropolis: A Study of Negro Life in the North*. New York: Harper and Row, 1962, revised and enlarged, 2 volumes.

DuBois, William E. B. *Economic Cooperation Among Negro Americans*. Atlanta: Atlanta University Press, 1907.

_____. *The Philadelphia Negro:* A Social Study. New York: Shocken Books, 1970 edition.

_____. *The Souls of Black Folk*. New American Library, 1969 edition.

Dybiec, David, editor. *Slippin' Away: The Loss of Black Owned Farms*. Atlanta: Glenmary Research Center, 1988.

Earl, Riggins R. *To You Who Teach in the Black Church*. Nashbville: National Baptist Publishing Board, 1972.

Edelin, Ramona H. "Curriculum and Cultural Identity" in *Infusion of African and African Amrican Content in the School Curriculum*. Asa Hilliard III, Lucretia Payton-Stewart and Larry Obadele Williams, editors. Morristown: Aaron Press, 1990.

Elizabeth. *Elizabeth, a Colored Minister of the Gospel Born in Slavery*. Philadelphia: Tract Association of Friends, 1889.

Felder, Cain Hope. *Stoney the Road We Trod*. Minneapolis: Fortress Press, 1971.

_____. *Troubling Biblical Waters*. Maryknoll: Orbis Books, 1989.

Felton, Carrol, Jr. "Harold Washington and the Value of Church and Community Development" in *The Black Church and the Harold Washington*

Story. Bristol: Wyndham Hall Press, 1988.

Felton, Ralph. *These My Brethren: A Study of 570 Negro Churches and 542 Negro Homes in the Rural South*. New York: Committee for the Training of the Negro Rural Pastors of the Phelps-Stokes Fund and the Home Missions Council of North America, 1950.

_____. *Go Down Moses: A Study of 21 Successful Negro Rural Pastors*. Madison, N.J.: Department of Rural Church, Drew Theological Seminary, 1952.

Fisher, Miles Mark. *Negro Slave Songs in the United States*. New York: Citadel, 1953.

Fitts, Leroy. *Lott Carey: First Black Missionary to Africa*. Valley Forge: Judson Press, 1978.

_____. *A History of Black Baptist*. Nashville: Broadman, 1985.

Foner, Philip S. (ed.) *W.E.B. DuBois Speaks*. New York: Pathfinder, 1970.

_____. *Business and Slavery: The New York Merchants and Their Repressible Conflict*. Chapel Hill: University of North Carolina Press, 1941.

Foster, William Z. *The Negro People in American History*. New York: International Publishers, 1954.

Freire, Paulo. *Pedagogy of the Oppressed*. New York: Orion, 1968.

Garvey, Amy Jacques. *The Philosophy and Opinions of Marcus Garvey*. Dover: The Majority Press, 1986.

Genovese, Eugene. *Roll, Jordan, Roll: The World the Slaves Made*. New York: Pantheon, 1974.

Gibson, Eugene. "Where Do We Go from Here?" in *The Black Church and the Harold Washington Story*. Bristol: Wyndham Hall Press, 1988.

Gibson, Harry. "Harold Washington and the Politics of Inclusiveness" in *The Black Church and the Harold Washington Story*. Bristol: Wyndham Hall Press, 1988.

Glazer, Nathan, and Daniel Patrick Moynihan. *Beyond the Melting Pot*. Cambridge, Massachusetts: MIT Press and Harvard University Press, 1963.

Gregg, Howard D. *Howard of the African Methodist Episcopal Church*. Chicago: University of Chicago Press, 1935.

Gutman, Herbert. *The Black Family in Slavery and Freedom, 1750-1925*. New York: Pantheon, 1976.

Hailey, Alex. *Roots: The Saga of an American Family*. Garden City, NJ: Doubleday, 1976.

Harding, Vincent. *There Is a River.* New York: Vintage Books, 1983.

Hardy, Henry. "Harold Washington Demonstrated That It Can Be Done" in *The Black Church and the Harold Washington Story.* Bristol: Wyndham Hall Press, 1988.

Harris, Joseph E. *Pillars in Ethiopian History.* Washington, D.C.: Howard University Press, 1974.

Henderson, Perry E. *The Black Church Credit Union.* Lima, Ohio: Fairway Press, 1990.

Hill, Robert. *The Strengths of Black Families.* New York: National Urban League, 1971.

Hilliard, Asa III, Lucretia Payton-Stewart and Larry Obadele Williams, editors. "A Reading Guide for the Study of Teaching of African World History" in *Infusion of African and African American Content in the School Curriculum.* Morristown: Aaron Press, 1990.

Hilliard, Clarence. "Black Evangelicalism and the Political Process as Reflected in the Harold Washington Story" in *The Black Church and the Harold Washington Story.* Bristol: Wyndham Hall Press, 1988.

Hopkins, Dwight. *Black Theology USA and South Africa: Politics, Culture, and Liberation.* Maryknoll: Orbis Books, 1990.

Hurston, Zora Neale. *The Sanctified Church.* Berkeley, California: Turtle Island, 1983.

Ibrahim, Hilmy. *The Literature of Egypt and the Sudan from the Earliest Times to the Year 1885.* London, 1886.

Jackson, Darrell, and A.P. Jackson. "Harold Washington and Martin Luther King, Jr." in *The Black Church and the Harold Washington Story.* Bristol: Wyndham Hall Press, 1988.

Jackson, Joseph H. *A Story of Christian Activism: The History of the National Baptist Convention, U.S.A., Inc.* Nashville: Townsend, 1980.

Jacobs, Sylvia M., editor. *Black Americans and the Missionary Movement in Africa.* Westport, Connecticut: Greenwood, 1982.

Jarrett, Nathaniel. "Toward a Ministry of Caring: Harold Washington and the Future of the Black Church" in *The Black Church and the Harold Washington Story.* Bristol: Wyndham Hall Press, 1988.

Johnson, Charles Spurgeon. *Growing Up in the Black Belt: Negro Youth in the Rural South.* New York: American Council on Education, 1941; reprint Schocken, 1967.

_____. *Shadow of the Plantation.* New York: Phoenix, 1966 reprint.

Johnson, Clifton H., editor. *God Struck Me Dead: Religious Conversion Ex-*

periences and Autobiographies of Ex-Slaves. Philadelphia: Pilgrim, 1960.

Johnson, Daniel M., and Rex Campbell. *Black Migration in America: A Social Demographic History*. Durham, N.C.: Duke University Press, 1981.

Jones, Marcus E. *Black Migration in the United States with Emphasis on Selected Central Cities*. Saratoga, CA.: Century Twenty-one Publishing, 1980.

Jordan, Charles Wesley. "The Role of the District Superintendent in the Harold Washington Story" in *The Black Church and the Harold Washington Story*. Bristol: Wyndham Hall Press, 1988.

Karenga, Maulana. *Introduction to Black Studies*. Los Angeles: University of Sankore Press, 1989.

Kotlowitz, Alex. *There Are No Children Here*. New York: Doubleday, 1991.

Lee, Jarena. *Religious Experience and Journal of Mrs. Jarena Lee*. Philadelphia: The author, 1849.

Lerner, Gerda. *Black Women in White America*. New York: Vintage Books, 1972.

BIOGRAPHIES

SERMONS

Elder David Birchett is the pastor of Christ Temple Apostolic Church in Marion, Indiana. He is the former State Youth President of the Northern District Council of the state of Michigan of the Pentecostal Assemblies of the World. He conducts revivals throughout the United States.

Bishop Charles Blake is bishop of the first Jurisdiction of Southern California of the Church of God in Christ, comprised of more than 250 churches. He is also on the board of 12 bishops of the Church of God in Christ International, and he is pastor of West Angeles Church of God in Christ in Los Angeles, California. He pastors more than 11,000 members. *Ebony's* 100+ Most Influential Black Americans, and former winners of *Ebony's* "Greatest Black Preacher" poll gave him honorable mention as one of the country's greatest Black preachers of 1993.

Dr. Delores Carpenter is the pastor of Michigan Park Christian Church, United Church of Christ, in Washington, D.C. She is associate professor of religious education at Howard University School of Divinity and was acting dean of academic affairs between 1991-1992. *Ebony's* 100+ Most Influential Black Americans, and former winners of *Ebony's* "Greatest Black Preacher" poll voted her among the greatest Black preachers of 1993.

Dr. David Hall is editor of the *Whole Truth* newspaper for the Church of God in Christ, based in Memphis, Tennessee. He serves on the publishing board of the Church of God in Christ, and he is the host of "Foundations of Pentecost" radio program, aired over WLMT radio station in Memphis, Tennessee. He is also the pastor of Temple Church of God in Christ in Memphis.

Dr. James Earl Massey is dean of the School of Theology at Anderson University in Anderson, Indiana. *Ebony's* 100+ Most Influential Black Americans, and former winners of *Ebony's* "Greatest Black Preacher" poll voted him among the country's greatest Black preachers of 1993.

Dr. Vashti McKenzie is the pastor of Payne Memorial African Methodist Episcopal Church in Baltimore, Maryland. She is the National Chaplain of Delta Sigma Theta Sorority, and is spiritual adviser for over 175,000 women. She is a former broadcast journalist and vice president of programming for WYCB in Washington, D.C., and she's had radio programs aired over WAYE, WEBB, and WJZ-TV in Baltimore, and over KATV in Oregon. She has written for a number of public daily and weekly newspapers, including the *Arizona Reporter* and the *Baltimore Afro-American*. She travels extensively, giving workshops and seminars and conducting revivals throughout the United States. *Ebony's* 100+ Most Influential Black Americans, and former winners of *Ebony's* "Greatest Black Preacher" poll voted her among the greatest Black preachers of 1993.

Rev. Frank Madison Reid is pastor of Bethel African Methodist Episcopal Church in Baltimore, Maryland, with pastoral responsibility for over 9,000 members. He has an "Outreach of Love" broadcast on Black Entertainment Television (BET) which airs to over 34 million viewers. He also broadcasts over the Armed Forces radio and television station, which airs in 123 countries and reaches over 1.5 million military personnel and civilians. He is the author of *The Nehemiah Plan,* a book about preparing the church to rebuild broken lives.

Rev. Paul Hobson Sadler, Sr. is the minister of Evangelism for African American and Native American Indian Church Development of the United Church of Christ, in Cleveland, Ohio. He is the former associate pastor of Trinity United Church of Christ and former pastor of Central Congregational Church in Louisiana. From 1988-1991 he was the host and executive producer of a weekly Christian talk show on cable television in New Orleans, Louisiana.

Rev. Sandra Sanford is a minister at Trinity United Church of Christ in Chicago, Illinois where Dr. Jeremiah A. Wright, Jr., is pastor.

Dr. J. Alfred Smith, Sr. is the senior pastor of Allen Temple Baptist Church in Oakland, California. In 1986-88, he was the president of the Progressive Baptist Convention. *Ebony's* 100+ Most Influential Black Americans and former winners of the "Greatest Black Preacher" poll voted Dr. Smith as one of the 15 greatest Black preachers in the United States for 1993.

Dr. Carlyle Stewart is the pastor of Hope United Methodist Church, in Southfield, Michigan.

Rev. Diana Timberlake is a minister at Trinity United Church of Christ in Chicago, Illinois where Dr. Jeremiah A. Wright, Jr. is pastor.

TESTIMONIES

Dr. Luther C. Benton, III of Midlothian, Virginia is a professor of theology at Richmond Virginia Seminary, and a food and milk consultant for the Commonwealth of Virginia. He is a minister in the Baptist church and preaches throughout the United States about the goodness of God.

Mother Esther Birchett went home to be with the Lord just before this book went to press. She was a member of Greater Grace Temple Apostolic Church in Detroit, Michigan, where Bishop David Ellis is pastor. She was a member of the Bishop's Choir, the Church Aide Society, Usher Board #2, the Women's Choir and the Missionary Department Circle #3.

Michael Jones is a member of Trinity United Church of Christ in Chicago, Illinois where Dr. Jeremiah A. Wright is pastor. He is employed by the church as a custodian.

Rev. George Liggins is the founder and pastor of Evangelistic Crusaders Church of God in Christ in Chicago, Illinois. He has pastored there for 20 years. He is an evangelistic and founder of missions in Haiti. His church provides the money for salaries for several teachers in schools in Haiti. His ministry helps the needy throughout the community surrounding his church.

Mrs. Maime Till-Mobley is the mother of Emmett Till, who was slain in August of 1955, about one year after the historic *Brown vs. Topeka Board of Education* decision desegregating schools in the South, during the height of the mid-20th century phase of the Civil Rights Movement. She is also the founder and director of the theater group, Emmett Till Players of Chicago, Illinois. She has received numerous awards for outstanding civic service, throughout the country. She has helped to found several churches in the Chicago metropolitan area, and she is one of the founding members of Evangelistic Crusaders Church of God in Christ where Rev. George Liggins is pastor.

Rev. Colleen Norman is a minister at Trinity United Church of Christ in Chicago, Illinois where Dr. Jeremiah A. Wright, Jr. is pastor. She is a former editor of the Vacation Bible School Series for Urban Ministries, Inc. of Chicago, Illinois.

Robert Rooker is a member of Joy Christian Fellowship Center in Chicago, Illinois. He recently had both of his legs amputated, but his faith is in God and his Spirit is high.

Vera Shelbon is a member of Allen Temple Baptist Church where Dr. J. Alfred Smith, Sr. is pastor. She belongs to the Women's Missionary Society, the Prayer Warriors, the Senior Citizens' Group, the April Birthday Club, and Pastor J. Alfred Smith's Bible class. She gives glory to God for all that God has done in her life.

Rev. Preston Smyth is an associate minister at Hope United Methodist Church in Southfield, Michigan where Dr. Carlyle Stewart is pastor. He is the founder of the "Can of Confidence" program which builds self-esteem and belief in young adults.

Rev. Ace Ware is an associate minister at Evangelistic Crusaders Church of God in Christ where Rev. George Liggins is pastor. He is formerly a commercial artist with extensive training in metallurgical research from the University of Chicago. He has been a minister for 43 years.